Learning VMware vRealize Automation

Learn the fundamentals of vRealize Automation
to accelerate the delivery of your IT services

Sriram Rajendran

BIRMINGHAM - MUMBAI

Learning VMware vRealize Automation

First published: January 2016

Production reference: 1280116

Published by Packt Publishing Ltd.
Livery Place
35 Livery Street
Birmingham B3 2PB, UK.

ISBN 978-1-78588-583-9

www.packtpub.com

Credits

Author
Sriram Rajendran

Reviewers
Sriram Balasubramanian
Kumaran Kamala Kannan
Sreekumar Nair
Aravind Sivaraman

Acquisition Editor
Rahul Nair

Content Development Editor
Samantha Gonsalves

Technical Editor
Tanmayee Patil

Copy Editor
Kausambhi Majumdar

Project Coordinator
Sanchita Mandal

Proofreader
Safis Editing

Indexer
Tejal Daruwale Soni

Graphics
Jason Monteiro

Production Coordinator
Aparna Bhagat

Cover Work
Aparna Bhagat

About the Author

Sriram Rajendran is a member of the CTO Ambassador program at VMware. He has been a veteran of the IT industry, for more than 12 years, and a focused technologist with expertise in cloud computing, networking, storage, and server virtualization technologies.

Sriram wears multiple hats at VMware. As a solution architect, he provides technical leadership and expertise to design, deploy, and scale the VMware SDDC stack for its Fortune 500 customers. His primary focus for VMware SSDC are automation, operations, and third-party integration.

As a senior escalations manager, he is the go-to person for handling critical executive escalations that have out blown traditional GSS escalation processes. His focus here is not just managing escalations through various internal VMware organizations but also external partner organizations and their processes and extranet multivendor support processes like TSANET.

As a CTO Ambassador, he is responsible for connecting the research and development team with customers, partners, and field as the global VMware evangelist. His focus is on defining and communicating VMware's vision and strategy, and acting as an advisor for VMware's vRealize Automation solutions, product roadmap, and portfolio.

Previously, as a staff escalation engineer, he worked on customer escalations and prioritizing the requests for the team. He was also the lead on recruitment and talent management for the support and escalations team. He also worked closely with various engineering teams within VMware to help provide early feedback on the design and architecture of products based on escalations and his other field interactions.

Prior to joining VMware, he worked at Slash Support and HP in their support organizations in technical leadership roles.

Sriram has devoted much of his professional career to the design, implementation, and maintenance of large physical and virtual networks, storage and servers, and cloud architectures based on VMware, Microsoft, and other leading enterprise technologies.

I would like to dedicate this book to my incredible parents, my wife, my siblings, and my friend—S.V. Rajendran, R. Mahalakshmi, Shwetha, Manju, Vani, Priya, Arunraj. Without your encouragement and support over so many years, this book would not have been possible.

About the Reviewers

Sriram Balasubramanian has over 17 years of experience in the IT field. He is currently working as a senior engineering manager for the VMware management business unit. In the last 6 years in VMware, he designed and developed various features for quite a few products such as vRealize Configuration Manager, vRealize Operations Management pack for vCloud Director, vRealize Orchestrator, and IT Financial Management. In his current capacity, he handles Fortune 500 critical customer escalations for management products.

Kumaran Kamala Kannan has over 5 years of experience in the IT field and holds a masters degree in network security. He is currently working as a senior member of the technical staff in VMware. He has worked on the development of multiple products including vRealize Configuration Manager, vRealize Orchestrator, and vRealize Automation. His research interests include computer and information security, cloud computing and data mining.

Sreekumar Nair has more than 10 years of experience in the IT industry with 6 years in VMware. He is currently working as a VMware technical account manager in Singapore, where he handles multiple critical customer accounts. Prior to this role, he was working as an escalation engineer with Global Support Services, where he handled escalations related to vRealize automation. Also, he has expertise in design and implementation of VMware infrastructure including automation solutions. He holds certifications from VMware, Microsoft, and, Citrix.

Aravind Sivaraman has over 9 years of experience in the IT field. He is currently working as a solution architect, providing the consultation, design, and delivery of complex IT infrastructure based on virtualization and cloud infrastructure solutions. He holds certifications from VMware, Microsoft, and Cisco, and has been awarded the VMware vExpert title for the last 3 years (2013-2015). He blogs at `http://www.aravindsivaraman.com/` and can be followed on Twitter at `@ss_aravind`.

He co-authored *VMware ESXi Cookbook* and was the technical reviewer of *Troubleshooting vSphere Storage, VMware vSphere Security Cookbook* and *VMware vSphere Design Essentials, Packt Publishing*.

www.PacktPub.com

Support files, eBooks, discount offers, and more

For support files and downloads related to your book, please visit www.PacktPub.com.

Did you know that Packt offers eBook versions of every book published, with PDF and ePub files available? You can upgrade to the eBook version at www.PacktPub.com and as a print book customer, you are entitled to a discount on the eBook copy. Get in touch with us at service@packtpub.com for more details.

At www.PacktPub.com, you can also read a collection of free technical articles, sign up for a range of free newsletters and receive exclusive discounts and offers on Packt books and eBooks.

https://www2.packtpub.com/books/subscription/packtlib

Do you need instant solutions to your IT questions? PacktLib is Packt's online digital book library. Here, you can search, access, and read Packt's entire library of books.

Why subscribe?

- Fully searchable across every book published by Packt
- Copy and paste, print, and bookmark content
- On demand and accessible via a web browser

Free access for Packt account holders

If you have an account with Packt at www.PacktPub.com, you can use this to access PacktLib today and view 9 entirely free books. Simply use your login credentials for immediate access.

Instant updates on new Packt books

Get notified! Find out when new books are published by following @PacktEnterprise on Twitter or the *Packt Enterprise* Facebook page.

Table of Contents

Preface

DynamicOps originated at Credit Suisse. Its software was initially developed at Credit Suisse's Global Research and Development Group in 2005 to help the company address the operational and governance challenges of rolling out virtualization technology. In 2008, after having deployed and used the software to manage thousands of its virtual machines, Credit Suisse decided to form a company based on the technology to form a new company—DynamicOps. Operations Virtualization is a foundational technology for DynamicOps' cloud offerings. Operations Virtualization is an abstraction layer between the multiple management systems that make up a cloud infrastructure and their consumers. It allows IT staff to apply management to the layers below without the layers above needing to know how or why. Later in July 2012, DynamicOps was acquired by VMware and the product was renamed to vCenter Automation Center (vCAC). With version 6.2 of vCAC, the product has been renamed to vRealize Automation (vRA) to align with their new strategies.

If there's one thing people should know about vRA, it's that it enables customers of any knowledge level to consume the cloud resources you give them access to. At the end of the day, customers don't care where a machine gets spun up as long as it's fast and it will do what they want. That means there's an approval in the request process, but then it goes off to one of the many hypervisor or cloud vendors we support. Imagine not having to put your cloud admins to work to build VMs daily, while at the same time they are getting deprovisioned automatically so that you don't have to buy hardware as often—that's the goal: ease of use for the customer, cost savings for the organization.

Today, the main value that vRA adds is the ability to manage and automate multiple cloud management tools (vSphere, RHEL KVM, AWS, and so on) as well as provision to physical hardware (through UCS, iDRAC, and iLO) to build manageable hybrid cloud, private cloud, virtual desktop, and platform as a service environments. That's a pretty large feat in itself, and you can bet that there are plans to add even more value to this product as it further integrates into the VMware suite of products.

What this book covers

Chapter 1, vRealize Automation and the Deconstruction of Components, intends to refresh your understanding with a succinct introduction to the vRealize automation architecture, and it depicts the high level details of every component involved.

Chapter 2, Distributed Installation Using Custom Certificates, implements and configures distributed architecture with custom certificates, which is a formidable task. While many blogs and official documentation talk about default installation, this chapter has the step-by-step illustrative recipe that will make it easy to follow and help you install and configure vRealize automation quickly and with a much better understanding.

Chapter 3, Functional Validation – Phase 1 and Installing Secondary Nodes, continues to install the remaining components in the distributed architecture; it will be worthwhile only if the installed components function out of the box. Once the setup is corroborated to be functional, we will advance and complete the installation.

Chapter 4, Configuring a Guest OS for vRealize Automation vSphere Blueprints, explains that the vRA blueprint can be created for different endpoints; this chapter will focus on the blueprint for the vSphere endpoint. Before we configure a blueprint for the vSphere endpoint, the vCenter-based templates need to go through a few configuration procedures. This is important for a successful deployment of the catalog items.

Chapter 5, Functional Validation – Phase 2 and Zero to VM Provisioning, spends time checking whether the setup is working as expected. While we deploy a service catalog item from the self-service user portal, we will discover the several stages of catalog deployment.

Chapter 6, Testing Failover Scenarios for vRealize Automation Components, explains that the job is not yet done once the installation and functional verification are successful. We'll spend time checking the failover scenarios for various components in this chapter.

Chapter 7, vRealize Orchestrator in High Availability via the NSX Load Balancer, focuses on the central topic of discussion in this chapter, which is the high availability configuration via NSX load balancer for vRealize Orchestrator. The Orchestrator cluster provides not only high availability, but also load balancing when configured with NSX or other third-party load balancer. We will delve into this in depth.

Chapter 8, The Power of Advanced Service Designer (ASD), provides the ability for service architects to create advanced services and publish them as catalog items. This provides the ability to create XaaS or *Anything as a Service* using VMware vRealize Orchestrator.

What you need for this book

This book covers a lot of ground and discusses the interactions with a lot of infrastructure services such as AD, DNS, Microsoft SQL Server, vSphere Infrastructure, NSX, vRealize Automation, and vRealize Orchestrator.

The bill of materials used in this book are, Windows 2012 AD, MS SQL 2008, vSphere 5.5 infrastructure, NSX 6.2 OVF, vRealize Automation 6.2 OVF, and Orchestrator 6.0 OVF. Also, you will need Windows 2008/2012 or a Linux distro of your choice (supported) for creating blueprints.

Who this book is for

This book is for anyone who wants to start their journey with vRealize Automation. It is your one-stop instruction guide to installing and configuring a distributed setup using NSX load balancer. Regardless of whether or not you have used vRealize Automation before, following the steps provided in each chapter will get you started with the product.

Conventions

In this book, you will find a number of text styles that distinguish between different kinds of information. Here are some examples of these styles and an explanation of their meaning.

Code words in text, database table names, folder names, filenames, file extensions, pathnames, dummy URLs, user input, and Twitter handles are shown as follows: "Log in to the publishing tenant portal (`https://CAFE.PKCt.LOCAL/vcac/org/Publishing`) as infrastructure administrator (`iadmin@pkct.local`)."

Any command-line input or output is written as follows:

```
Listing queues...
Error: unable to connect to node rabbit@localhost: nodedown
```

New terms and **important words** are shown in bold. Words that you see on the screen, for example, in menus or dialog boxes, appear in the text like this: "Navigate to **Infrastructure | Monitoring | Distributed Execution Status**."

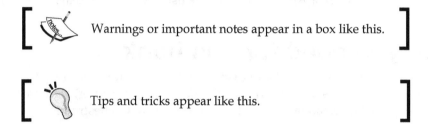

Warnings or important notes appear in a box like this.

Tips and tricks appear like this.

Reader feedback

Feedback from our readers is always welcome. Let us know what you think about this book—what you liked or disliked. Reader feedback is important for us as it helps us develop titles that you will really get the most out of.

To send us general feedback, simply e-mail feedback@packtpub.com, and mention the book's title in the subject of your message.

If there is a topic that you have expertise in and you are interested in either writing or contributing to a book, see our author guide at www.packtpub.com/authors.

Customer support

Now that you are the proud owner of a Packt book, we have a number of things to help you to get the most from your purchase.

Downloading the example code

You can download the example code files from your account at http://www.packtpub.com for all the Packt Publishing books you have purchased. If you purchased this book elsewhere, you can visit http://www.packtpub.com/support and register to have the files e-mailed directly to you.

Downloading the color images of this book

We also provide you with a PDF file that has color images of the screenshots/ diagrams used in this book. The color images will help you better understand the changes in the output. You can download this file from http://www.packtpub. com/sites/default/files/downloads/LearningVMwarevRealizeAutomation_ ColorImages.pdf.

Errata

Although we have taken every care to ensure the accuracy of our content, mistakes do happen. If you find a mistake in one of our books—maybe a mistake in the text or the code—we would be grateful if you could report this to us. By doing so, you can save other readers from frustration and help us improve subsequent versions of this book. If you find any errata, please report them by visiting http://www.packtpub. com/submit-errata, selecting your book, clicking on the **Errata Submission Form** link, and entering the details of your errata. Once your errata are verified, your submission will be accepted and the errata will be uploaded to our website or added to any list of existing errata under the Errata section of that title.

To view the previously submitted errata, go to https://www.packtpub.com/books/ content/support and enter the name of the book in the search field. The required information will appear under the **Errata** section.

Piracy

Piracy of copyrighted material on the Internet is an ongoing problem across all media. At Packt, we take the protection of our copyright and licenses very seriously. If you come across any illegal copies of our works in any form on the Internet, please provide us with the location address or website name immediately so that we can pursue a remedy.

Please contact us at copyright@packtpub.com with a link to the suspected pirated material.

We appreciate your help in protecting our authors and our ability to bring you valuable content.

Questions

If you have a problem with any aspect of this book, you can contact us at questions@packtpub.com, and we will do our best to address the problem.

1
vRealize Automation and the Deconstruction of Components

Welcome to the world of automation! I am sure you have heard about **vRealize Automation** product (**vRA**), formerly **vCloud Automation Center** (**vCAC**). In this chapter, we will focus on the use cases and what vRealize Automation solution is. We will further discuss the following topics:

- The conceptual diagram of vRealize Automation
- CAFÉ Appliance and component deep dive
    - vPostgres
    - RabbitMQ
    - vCAC server
    - tcServer (Tomcat)
    - Telemetry

- IaaS – architecture and component deep dive

    - Model Manager Web (a.k.a. repository)
    - Model Manager Data
    - MSSQL database
    - Manager Service
    - DEM (Orchestrator and Worker)
    - Proxy agents
    - Management agents (starting vRA 6.2)

What is vRealize Automation?

vRealize Automation (a.k.a vRA) is a complete **Cloud Management Platform** (**CMP**) that can be used to build and manage a multi-vendor cloud infrastructure. Using an automation solution, end users can self-provision virtual machines in private and public cloud environments, physical machines (install OEM images), applications, and IT services according to policies defined by administrators.

Using a sales pitch definition—it is a self-serviced, policy-driven orchestration and cloud automation engine with integration capabilities built into the core of the product.

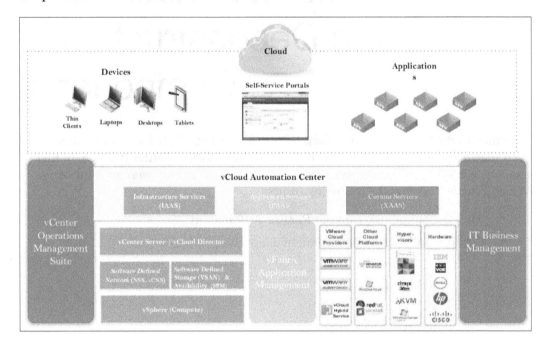

Before you move forward, I would like you to take a closer look at the preceding image that depicts how various products in VMware dovetail to complement the automation solution. The automation construct is built upon a layer of management that can automate tasks and activities in *compute*, *storage*, and *network* components that is referred to as **Software-Defined Data Center** (**SDDC**).

Key capabilities

I have listed a few key capabilities about vRealize Automation. While there could be many more, the following list should cover it all:

- A single solution of abstracted service models
- Model once, deploy anywhere
- Personalization through policies

A single solution of abstracted service models

vRealize Automation provides the ability to create models of services. These services are abstracted from each other within a single solution. For example, application services (PaaS) are abstracted from infrastructure services (IaaS), which are further abstracted from resource pools. I like to think about these as layers of services, layered on top of each other like the layers of an onion. If you think about it, VMware has always been in the business of providing abstraction.

Model once – deploy anywhere

The power of the abstracted service model is that you can treat a model the same irrespective of where the service gets deployed. You can model a service once, and deploy it anywhere; be it production or development or a cloud (private or public) setup.

Personalization through policies (governance)

Governance is considered a high priority item in the world of automation. Even though we want to create models of abstracted services that can be treated the same irrespective of where they get deployed, we do not want to provide each consumer with the same service. Each consumer demands a personalized service for specific business needs. vRealize Automation provides this ability through policies. Fine-grained policies work in conjunction with personalization of a service. For example, if a developer requests a service, they will receive a development environment with a small footprint, without the need for approvals, perhaps deployed into the public cloud. If a business analyst requests the same service, their personalized service may get deployed into the private cloud by placing approvals in place.

These key capabilities of vRealize Automation are unique. They are critical for providing agility by automating the delivery of personalized services.

Common use cases of vRealize Automation

From my experience, here are the most common use cases of vRealize Automation solution:

- Create a catalog of standard operating systems that can be consumed by an organization with a single click

- Offer other services beyond infrastructure, for example — PaaS, XaaS

- Requirement to integrate with CMDB or ITSM tools to track activities about a machine when it's provisioned

- The integration of an IPAM system for an IP address when provisioning a machine

- Advanced governance is priority

- Hybrid cloud deployments

Many other use cases can be listed here, but I will limit the list since our primary requirement is to make you understand the core capabilities of the product.

Do spend some time to recognize the goodness this product has:

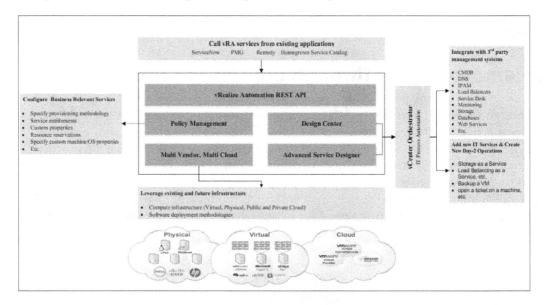

vRealize Automation – a conceptual diagram

Just for the ease of understanding, we have broken down the components of vRealize Automation into the following:

- An identity source used for authentication (can be a Windows- or Linux-based identity management server)
- A vRealize Automation appliance, a.k.a. a **Cloud Automation Framework for Extensibility (CAFÉ)** appliance
- An IaaS server

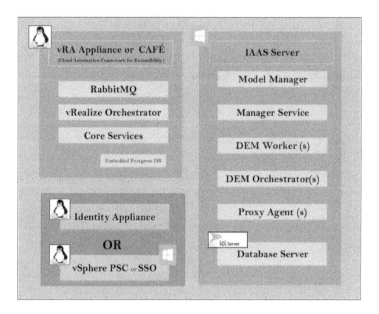

Identity management appliance or SSO or PSC

The identity management appliance or vSphere 5.5 SSO or vSphere 6.0 PSC provides **Single Sign-On (SSO)** capabilities that allow connectivity to **Active Directory (AD)** or Open LDAP-compatible directory services.

Identity management appliance

This is a preconfigured virtual appliance that serves as the heart of the SSO system with limited capabilities released specifically for the vRealize Automation product. It serves all authentication requests and handles multiple identity sources and uses a routing layer to route requests to an appropriate subsystem (a configuration or authentication interface). It is important to note that an IDM appliance is recommended for small-scale deployments. If your design demands high availability, you could use a vSphere feature such as HA and FT since the IDM appliance does not have native capability to cluster or join with the existing SSO deployments.

vSphere 5.5 SSO

vSphere 5.5 SSO is available as a Windows-based as well as a Linux-based appliance and can be added to an existing SSO domain. If your design demands an SSO configuration to be highly available behind a load balancer, you are limited to using only a Windows version of SSO, but be aware that it supports active/passive failover mode.

vSphere 6.0 PSC

Since the release of vSphere 6, the SSO configuration has been built into **Platform Service Controller (PSC)** that is available in both Linux and Windows-based flavor. If your design demands an SSO configuration to be highly available behind a load balancer, you have the flexibility to choose between both Linux and Windows:

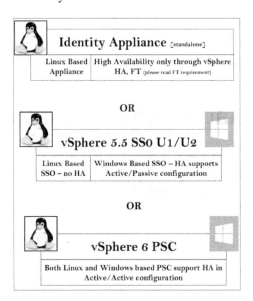

vRealize Automation or CAFÉ appliance

A vRealize Automation or CAFÉ appliance is a preconfigured virtual appliance that deploys vRealize Automation services and related components. The virtual appliance is built on top of the **SUSE Linux Enterprise Server** 11 (**SLES**) operating system. The CAFÉ appliance is focused on the business logic behind vRA that allows the IaaS component to focus on provisioning.

The server includes the vRealize Automation services, which provide the following:

- A single portal for self-service provisioning
- The management of cloud services
- Authoring and administration
- Governance-related tasks

It includes an embedded vPostgres database, vRealize Orchestrator (server/configurator), Rabbit MQ messaging server, and vFabric Tomcat server:

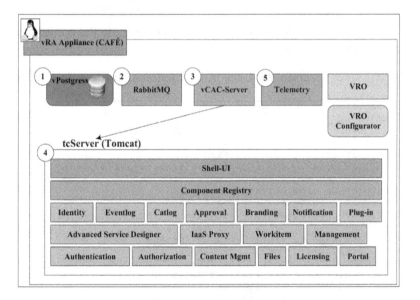

vPostgres

The CAFÉ appliance has an embedded vPostgres database for catalog persistence. This appliance has the option to either use the embedded Postgres database or an external vPostgres database. Some of the contents of the database include the following:

- Catalog item details
- Entitlements

- Approval policies
- Advanced Service Designer information
- Service definitions

RabbitMQ

This is a message broker that uses the **Advanced Message Queuing Protocol** (**AMQP**). Since RabbitMQ service will start before the vcac-server service, it is important that RabbitMQ service starts successfully; otherwise, some of the vRA services will fail. While the services in the CAFÉ appliance use REST API to communicate with each other, RabbitMQ is used to handle the following:

- Work queues

- Buffer and batch operations

- Request offloading

- Workload distribution

To check whether the RabbitMQ server is connected, execute the command as shown in the screenshot in the vRealize Automation server — `rabbitmqctl list_queues`.

If the RabbitMQ server is connected, the output will match the following screenshot:

```
CAFE1:~ # rabbitmqctl list_queues
Listing queues ...
vmware.vcac.core.approval-service.approvalProcessor      0
vmware.vcac.core.approval-service.approvalUpdater        0
vmware.vcac.core.approval-service.error 0
vmware.vcac.core.cache.queue.identity.cafe.node.451376077.918     0
vmware.vcac.core.cache.queue.workitem-service.cafe.node.451376077.918    0
vmware.vcac.core.catalog-service.error   0
vmware.vcac.core.catalog-service.notification    0
vmware.vcac.core.catalog-service.requestApproved        0
vmware.vcac.core.catalog-service.requestCompleted       0
vmware.vcac.core.catalog-service.requestPostApproved    0
vmware.vcac.core.catalog-service.requestSubmitted       0
vmware.vcac.core.catalog-service.retryRequestApproved   0
vmware.vcac.core.catalog-service.retryRequestCompleted  0
vmware.vcac.core.catalog-service.retryRequestSubmitted  0
vmware.vcac.core.catalog-service.rollbackRequest        0
vmware.vcac.core.identity.error 0
vmware.vcac.core.notification-service.email      0
vmware.vcac.core.notification-service.error      0
vmware.vcac.core.notification-service.inboundMessage     0
vmware.vcac.core.notification-service.notification       0
vmware.vcac.core.notification-service.notificationCallback       0
vmware.vcac.core.notification-service.notificationCallbackError 0
vmware.vcac.core.workitem-service.delegates      0
vmware.vcac.core.workitem-service.error 0
vmware.vcac.core.workitem-service.notification   0
CAFE1:~ #
```

In case the RabbitMQ server is down, the result will be an error as shown:

```
Listing queues...
Error: unable to connect to node rabbit@localhost: nodedown
```

vCAC server

This service is the core of vRealize Automation. It starts the tcServer component when it is initialized.

tcServer (Tomcat)

VMware vFabric tcServer is a web application server based on open source Apache Tomcat. With its lean architecture and small memory footprint, tcServer requires significantly fewer resources than conventional Tomcat servers and allows you to have a greater server density in virtual and cloud environments. vRealize Automation deploys all the web applications inside the vFabric tcServer:

```
CAFE1:/var/lib/vcac/server/webapps # ls -lhrt
total 84K
drwxr-xr-x   6 root root 4.0K May 20 22:32 advanced-designer-service
drwxr-xr-x   4 root root 4.0K May 20 22:32 ROOT
drwxr-xr-x   5 root root 4.0K May 20 22:32 branding-service
drwxr-xr-x   5 root root 4.0K May 20 22:32 approval-service
drwxr-xr-x   6 root root 4.0K May 20 22:32 catalog-service
drwxr-xr-x   5 root root 4.0K May 20 22:32 identity
drwxr-xr-x   6 root root 4.0K May 20 22:32 iaas-proxy-provider
drwxr-xr-x   5 root root 4.0K May 20 22:32 eventlog-service
drwxr-xr-x   4 root root 4.0K May 20 22:32 console-proxy-service
drwxr-xr-x   5 root root 4.0K May 20 22:32 component-registry
drwxr-xr-x   6 root root 4.0K May 20 22:32 management-service
drwxr-xr-x   4 root root 4.0K May 20 22:32 socialcast-plugin
drwxr-xr-x   5 root root 4.0K May 20 22:32 reservation-service
drwxr-xr-x   5 root root 4.0K May 20 22:32 notification-service
drwxr-xr-x   5 root root 4.0K May 20 22:32 workitem-service
drwxr-xr-x  11 root root 4.0K May 20 22:32 vcac
drwxr-xr-x   6 root root 4.0K May 20 22:33 artifact-management-service
drwxr-xr-x   6 root root 4.0K May 20 22:33 release-management-service
drwxr-xr-x   5 root root 4.0K May 20 22:33 dashboard-service
drwxr-xr-x   5 root root 4.0K May 20 22:33 resource-service
drwxr-xr-x   5 root root 4.0K May 20 22:33 files-service
CAFE1:/var/lib/vcac/server/webapps # _
```

- **Shell-UI**: This is the web interface that users hit when they connect to the CAFÉ UI.

- **Component registry**: This is similar to the SSO lookup service in vCenter. It acts as a central repository that manages all the common services and endpoints. Since all services are registered to component registry, a lookup is performed against it to find the URI and its certificates.

  ◦ A central repository for all the services and stores endpoint-related information

  ◦ A central repository for clients to get the required service and endpoint information

  ◦ A central repository that provides the health status of every service — checks whether a service is alive or dead

Telemetry

Telemetry was introduced with the vRealize Automation 6.2 version and is also known as the **Customer Experience Improvement Program** (CEIP). The intent of this new feature is to allow customers to *opt-in* to send information back to VMware for the purpose of improving the product. This functionality lives within the CAFÉ appliance and is turned off by default when the VA is deployed. To access it, you will have to navigate to the vRA VA VAMI page and click the new tab called **Telemetry**. Within this screen, you can set when and how often the data is sent back to VMware along with any sort of data masking rules that you want to set up.

IaaS – architecture and component deep dive

vRA IaaS is made up of several components, and it is important to understand how they all relate to each other. The following conceptual diagram will help to illustrate what is being installed on the Windows Server:

- Model Manager Web (a.k.a. repository)
  ◦ IaaS Web UI
  ◦ WAPI
  ◦ Reports

- Model Manager Data
- MSSQL database
- Manager Service

- DEM (orchestrator and worker)
- Proxy agents
- Management agents (starting with vRA 6.2)

All of the preceding components will be installed in Windows OS:

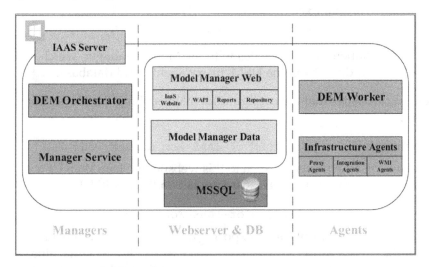

Model Manager

The Model Manager role actually refers to two types of data—*Model Manager Data* and *Model Manager Web* a.k.a. *repository*.

Model Manager Data

The Model Manager Data holds the business logic required to connect/manage endpoints and execute workflows.

Since the business logic is uploaded to the database during the installation of the first web node, the successive web node installation in a distributed install does not allow us to install the Model Manager Data.

Please note, the business logic is always referenced from the database and never referenced from the Model Manager Data folder stored in the filesystem of first web node. While the business logic is not referenced during runtime, it is used only during upgrades or when executing the Register Solution User and **RepoUtil** commands.

Model Manager Web a.k.a. repository

Model Manager is designed for Microsoft IIS and therefore, needs to be installed on a Microsoft IIS Web Server. Model Manager Web is also referred to as repository. It exposes the IaaS data model as a service and allows **Create/Read/Update/Delete (CRUD)** operations on the IaaS database. They implement the business logic that is executed by **Distributed Execution Manager (DEM)** — this triggers DEM workflows (more details later in this chapter) on create/update/delete.

The website component communicates with the Model Manager, which provides the component with updates from the DEM, proxy agents, and database.

There are four websites that are configured while installing the Model Manager Web component:

- **IaaS Web UI**: `https://FQDN-of-IAAS-Web-Server/vcac`

  When a user requests to log in to this website, the IaaS Web UI presents the form in a frame on the **Infrastructure** tab on the CAFÉ UI.

- **WAPI portal**: `https://FQDN-of-IAAS-Web-Server/WAPI`

  This is a IIS web application exposing a private API through a REST interface. Web API is a proxy layer that exists in the web machine, which is a service-oriented API developed using .NET, and acts as the integration point between the CAFÉ appliance and the repository. WAPI is registered in the component registry against the IaaS service. The important point to note is that the vCAC service uses the WAPI endpoint registered in component registry to communicate with IaaS components. WAPI is also used to check the *health* status of the IaaS service. In short, all communication for IIS goes through WAPI.

- **Reporting website**: `https://FQDN-of-IaaS-Web-Server/vcacReports`

  As the name suggests, it is used for any reporting-related information.

- **Repository website**: `https://FQDN-of-IaaS-Server/Repository`

  Connecting to this website will fetch you the details related to the repository. However, the only catch is that you should connect to the nodes (`WEB1` or `WEB2`) directly and not via the load balancer virtual IP.

MSSQL database

This database is used by the IaaS component to store the following:

- Business groups

- Fabric groups

- Endpoint definitions

- IaaS resources

- Reservation policies

- Blueprints

 Microsoft Distributed Transaction Coordinator (MSDTC) must be enabled in the database machine. The only supported high availability model for the database is through Windows Server Failover Clustering, and this requires a shared block storage. The newer Always On replication model is not supported today due to the vRA dependency of the MSDTC but it does not work with Always On.

Manager Service

The vCloud Automation Center service (commonly called the Manager Service) is a Windows .NET service that coordinates communication between DEMs, agents including guest agents (over SOAP), the IaaS database, AD (or LDAP), and SMTP. The Manager Service communicates with the repository to queue external workflows in the SQL database that will be later picked up by either a DEM worker or a proxy agent or a guest agent.

Some of the key functionalities of Manager Services are listed here:

- Triggers inventory/state/performance data collection for the managed compute resource.

- Processes data collection response ONLY for *proxy agent-based hypervisor*.

- The master workflows (machine transition states from requested to destroy) are handled by Manager Service. For details on the life cycle states, refer the following diagram:

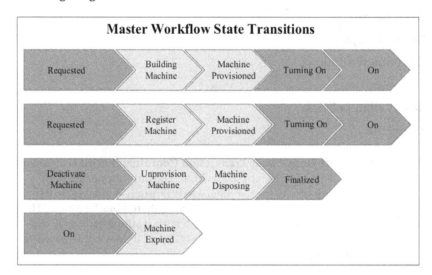

Master Workflow State Transitions

[The grayed-out states give extensibility hooks.]

A **Virtual Machine Observer (VMO)** task is another important task performed by Manager Service. This task is scheduled to be executed every 60 minutes to check whether any machine has expired or reached the archive state and initiates the required operations. Earlier, in the vRA 6.2 version, a VMO task was executed every 10 seconds. Since it's a resource-intensive action, it has been added as a configuration parameter in the manager service config file (`ProcessLeaseWorkflowTimerCallbackIntervalMiliSeconds`).

For additional details, please refer to `http://pubs.vmware.com/vra-62/index.jsp?topic=%2Fcom.vmware.vra.system.administration.doc%2FGUID-5FBB7C73-2AAD-4106-9C0D-DE7B416A4716.html`.

Distributed Execution Manager

The **Distributed Execution Manager (DEM)** is of two types. It can either act as a DEM Worker or a DEM Orchestrator.

DEM Orchestrator (DEO)

One of the main tasks of a DEM Orchestrator is to monitor the status and health of DEM Workers:

- If the Worker service stops or loses its connection to the repository (Model Manager Web), the DEM Orchestrator clears all associated workflow instances to the non-functional DEM Worker, thus allowing the other DEM Workers to pick up the workflows. This explains why we don't need to explicitly create high availability for DEM workers.

- Performs the scheduling of daily recurring workflows, such as inventory data collections, state data collection, and performance collections, by creating new workflow instances at the scheduled time.

- The **RunOneOnly** feature in the DEM Orchestrator ensures that only one instance of any workflow is executed at a given time by the DEM Worker.

- It pre-processes workflows before they are executed including checking the preconditions that are required for the workflows.

- From an availability standpoint, the DEM Orchestrator works in an active/ standby configuration. At least one DEM Orchestrator is necessary every time workflows are run. It's also recommended to install an additional DEM Orchestrator instance on a separate machine to help in providing HA in case of failure. In case of failure in the active DEM Orchestrator, the standby Orchestrator will take over automatically since it monitors the status of the active DEM Orchestrator.

DEM Worker

Distributed Execution Manager (DEM) Worker executes the core business logic of custom models by interacting with the VMware database and with systems such as **vRealize Orchestrator (vRO)**, **vCloud Director**, and **vCloud Air** . Multiple DEMs can be deployed for scalability, availability, and distribution. DEMs can also manage physical machine-related life cycle events.

Infrastructure agent

The agents are designed to interact with external systems. There are different types of agents, each having specific functions:

- **Virtualization proxy agents**: These interact with hypervisors (vSphere, KVM, Hyper-V) to provision virtual machines and the data collection of an inventory. There can be multiple proxy agents to the same hypervisor (*N: 1*).

- **Integration agents**: **Virtual desktop integration (VDI)** and **external provisioning integration (EPI)** fall under this purview.
- **WMI agents**: These enable data collection from the Windows machines managed by vRealize Automation.

If you have more than one vCenter endpoint, then you have to install an additional vSphere agent—it's a 1:1 mapping between the vCenter endpoint and the vSphere Agent. You can have multiple agents talking to the same vCenter endpoint in case of high availability but each agent should be on a different server, and they all should have the same name else you will run into many issues. For example if you have three agents pointing to a single vCenter Server, then all the three agents pointing to this vCenter Server should be named as *Agent*. Please refer to *KB: 2052062* for additional details.

Management agent

The management agent helps to collect *support* and *telemetry* log information through a cluster collection process. The management agent is automatically installed as a part of deployment in every IaaS node. The management agent pings the CAFÉ appliance via port 5480 every three minutes to check whether any work item (telemetry information or a log bundle collection) is pending. If a work item is pending, it will execute the work item and send back the response. So even if the vCAC server service in the CAFÉ appliance has been stopped, the management agent will be able to function.

The roadmap for the management agent in the upcoming releases of vRA will be the following:

- Enable vRealize Automation to automate the installation of IaaS components (Windows-based)
- Can be installed via command line or UI

Startup order

As you have understood that the vRealize Automation solution has multiple components, the startup order for every component plays an important role when recovering from a power outage or an orchestrated shutdown. Here is the recommended startup method.

Start with the load balancer; ensure that it is fully functional before moving on to the next step. If NSX LB is used, connect to the NSX Edge appliance via SSH and execute the command (`show service loadbalancer monitor`) and check whether the configuration is intact and enabled:

1. Power on the PostgreSQL and MSSQL database machines if external to your servers. If embedded with the CAFÉ nodes, these must come up first in the boot order.

2. Power on the identity appliance or vSphere SSO/PSC, and wait until the startup finishes. Before moving on to the next step, do the following:

   1. Connect to the SSO/PSC web portal using its virtual IP (only for SSO and PSC, if they are behind a load balancer). For example, `https://psc.pkct.local` (this should take you to the SSO/PSC page).

   2. For the identity appliance, connect to the VAMI page. For example, `https://FQDN-of-Identify-Appliance:5480`

3. Power on the primary vRealize Appliance. If you are running a distributed deployment, start the secondary virtual appliances next and wait until the startup finishes.

4. Power on vRealize Orchestrator. If you are running a distributed deployment, start the secondary appliances next and wait until the startup finishes.

5. Power on the primary web node and wait until the startup finishes:

   1. If you are running a distributed deployment, start all the secondary web nodes.

6. Power on all the Manager Service nodes.

7. Power on the Distributed Execution Manager Orchestrator, Workers, and all vRealize Automation agents.

8. You can start these components in any order and you do not need to wait for one startup to finish before you start another.

Once all these steps are completed, perform the following steps:

1. In a simple deployment—`https://FQDN-or-IP-of-CAFE:5480/` and wait until all the services show up as **REGISTERED**.

2. In a distributed deployment—`https://FQDN-or-IP-of-CAFÉ(1/2..n):5480` and wait until all the services show up as **REGISTERED**.

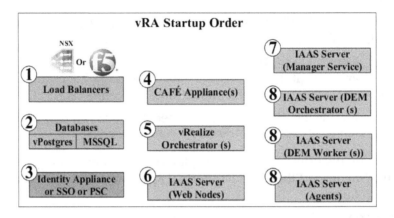

Shutdown order

To preserve data integrity, follow the following shutdown order for the vRealize Automation components:

1. Shut down the primary vRO appliance. Once the shutdown completes, shut down the secondary nodes.

2. Shut down the Distributed Execution Manager Orchestrator, Workers, and all the vRealize Automation agents in any order and wait until all components finish shutting down.

3. Shut down the Manager Service machine. Once the shutdown finishes, continue to shut down additional nodes if they exist.

4. Shut down the primary web node. Once the shutdown finishes, continue to shut down additional nodes if they exist.

5. Shut down the primary vRealize CAFÉ appliance. Once the shutdown finishes, continue to shut down additional node if they exist.

6. Shut down the PostgreSQL and MSSQL virtual machines in any order and wait until the shutdown finishes.

7. Shut down your SSO appliance, which could be an identity appliance or a vSphere SSO/PSC if this is dedicated for the vRA deployment.

8. Shutting down the load balancer will be the last step.

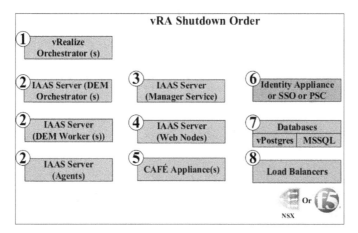

Summary

This chapter is intended to refresh your understanding of the vRA architecture, and it depicts the high level details of every component involved. It's important for us to understand the functionality of each component and its workflow before we set out to build the distributed vRealize Automation installation. In the next chapter, we will focus on planning the requirements and steps involved in building the distributed vRealize Automation infrastructure.

Distributed Installation Using Custom Certificates

Deploying and configuring distributed architecture using custom certificates is unarguably a challenging task. In this chapter, we will focus on step-by-step elucidative material that will be easy to follow and guide you through the installation faster.

This chapter is precisely an installation guide that will help users deploy vRA in a distributed architecture. Our focus will be around the installation, configuration of vRA components, and configuration of NSX load balancer settings. It is assumed that the infrastructure setups (Active Directory, DNS, vRA hostname and IP address, NSX Manager, and Edge) are deployed, configured, and supported to work properly in the target environment.

The following topics will be covered in this chapter:

- Planning and preparing for the installation
- An overview of the installation flow
- Identity management for authentication and authorization by vRA components
- Identity appliance configuration
- NSX load balancer configuration
- Configuring external vPostgres DB in HA for the vRealize Automation CAFÉ appliance

- Configuring the CAFÉ appliance in HA

- IaaS installation

- Installation of a first manager service and DEM orchestrator node

- Installation of the first DEM Worker and proxy agent

- Proxy agent installation

Getting started

From an architecture standpoint, deployment modes can be of two types—simple and distributed.

Simple deployment architecture

As the name suggests, a simple installation deploys a single instance of each virtual appliance and installs all IaaS components, including the SQL database, in a single virtual machine. It is highly suited for development or proof-of-concept environments. Importantly, this deployment lacks high availability.

Distributed deployment architecture

A distributed installation allows the separation of components that are best suited to the organization's needs and ideally used in production environments, and provides options for high availability. We have three distinct deployment modes: small, medium, and large. To learn more about these deployment modes, refer to `http://www.vmware.com/files/pdf/products/vCloud/VMware-vCloud-Automation-Center-61-Reference-Architecture.pdf`.

Planning and preparation

Here are some of the key tasks to do before we start the actual implementation:

- **Download the software**: VMware OVA (CAFÉ, NSX) and third-party software will be required; download it on a file share within the target data center.

- **Hostname and IP address planning**: Based on your enterprise naming convention, list the hostname and IP address for each component, including the virtual IP in load balancer.

- **SSL certificate generation**: vRealize Automation (vRA product requires the use of *signed certificates*. Windows **AD Certificate Services**, or **ADCS**, are acceptable). We will leverage a certification generation tool for this task. The reference is `kb.vmware.com/kb/2107816`.

- **Create DNS entries**: FQDNs will be used throughout our installation. Windows VMs will self-register if a Windows-based DNS is used. Manually create the *A* record (*forward lookup*) and *PTR* record (*reverse lookup*) for Linux-based VMware virtual appliances and load balancer virtual addresses.

- **Create service account**: Create an Active Directory domain account, and it's extremely important to set the password to never expire.

- **Load balancer configuration**: The commonly used one-armed load balancer topology will be configured. Create node entries, virtual addresses (VIPs), and health monitors prior to the installation.

- **Microsoft SQL Server**: vRA IaaS components require MSSQL. Windows failover clustering is desirable in order to meet availability objectives.

Infrastructure details

Before we begin the installation journey, it is good practice to decide on the hostnames and IP addresses for the services that will be used. I have created a simple table for your reference as the hostnames will be used in throughout this book. Use this table to create the DNS entries as they will be required during and after installation:

Hostname	IP address	Service
vIDM	10.0.0.110	Identity management
vPG	10.0.0.111	Virtual IP for Postgres in a load balancer
PG1	10.0.0.112	First Postgres node
PG2	10.0.0.113	Second Postgres node
CAFÉ	10.0.0.114	Virtual IP for CAFÉ in a load balancer
CAFE1	10.0.0.115	First CAFÉ node
CAFE2	10.0.0.116	Second CAFÉ node
WEB	10.0.0.117	Virtual IP for IaaS web (model manager) in a load balancer
WEB1	10.0.0.118	First WEB node
WEB2	10.0.0.119	Second WEB node
MGR	10.0.0.120	Virtual IP for IaaS manager service in the load balancer

Hostname	IP address	Service
MGR1	10.0.0.121	First manager service plus DEM Orchestrator node
MGR2	10.0.0.122	Second manager service + DEM Orchestrator node
WRK1	10.0.0.123	First DEM Worker + proxy agent node
WRK2	10.0.0.124	Second DEM Worker + proxy agent node

 In our design, DEM Orchestrator will be installed along with the manager service in the same node. The proxy agent will be installed in the same node as the DEM worker.

Distributed architecture

To ensure business continuity, we are seeing umpteen customers implement vRealize Automation (vRA) in a highly available configuration. In this book, we will talk about the step-by-step instructions on how to configure and implement the following architecture. Before you start debating the design, let me set the stage here:

- The MSSQL cluster is beyond the scope of this book, and it's assumed that you have already taken care of it. From the product requirement perspective, MSDTC should be configured in the SQL machine before installing IaaS components.

- As you progress through reading this book, we will discuss the reasons behind our design approach for each component.

- For now, take a deep look at this architecture to understand the communication flow at a high level and the ports used:

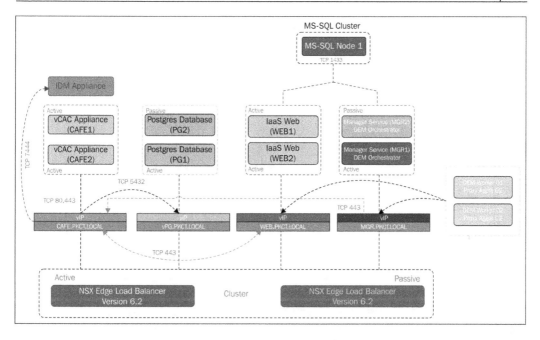

Bill of materials

The inventory and specifications of components that comprise vRealize Automation are provided here:

- vRealize Automation version 6.2.2 | Build 2754336
- Identity management version 2.2.2.0 | Build 2755560
- NSX Manager 6.2 | Build 2986609
- All IaaS components will be installed on a virtual machine
- Windows OS—Windows 2012 Standard
- Database—SQL Server 2008 R2 RTM (10.50.1600.1) Enterprise Edition (x64)
- vSphere 6.0

Overview of the installation flow

I have put together a flowchart in the hope that it helps you recognize the high-level steps involved in building a distributed and highly available vRealize Automation infrastructure.

The following steps are detailed in a logical sequence that takes dependencies into account:

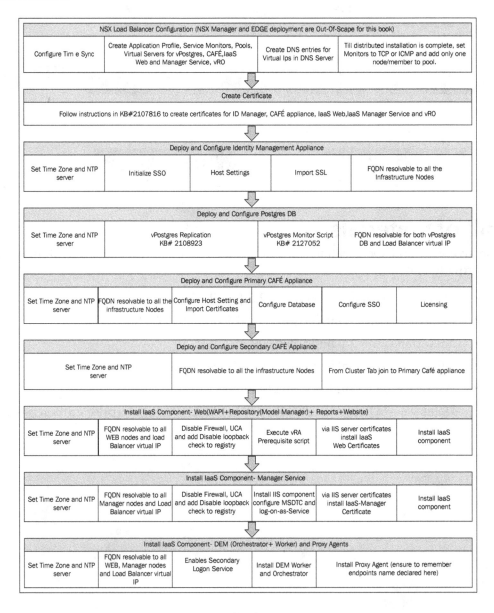

Certificates

SSL certificates are commonly used for a secure handshake between different services. In vRA, all communications between the client browser and services (identity management, CAFÉ, and IaaS) and between services are over TLS/SSL. However, I wanted to highlight that vRA components work with different SSL certificate file formats. Here is a list of the common formats used in a vRA solution:

- **PEM**: short for Privacy Enhanced Mail
- **P7B**: **Public Key Cryptography Standard (PKCS)** Format #7
- **PFX**: **Public Key Cryptography Standard (PKCS)** Format #12
- **CSR**: short for Certificate Signing Request (`.CER` or `.CRT` files can be in either PEM or DER format):

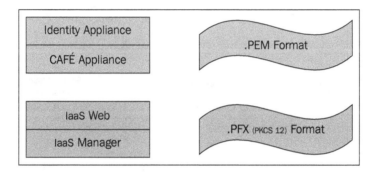

The certificate generation process

Given that certificate generation is a protracted process, we have detailed the high-level steps involved in creating the certificates. The extensive list of steps for creating the certificates will be covered later in this chapter:

Step 1:

- Download the Certgen script from `http://kb.vmware.com/kb/2107816` and upload it to a Linux appliance (IDM, since it will be deployed first).
- Create a file called `servers.txt` in the same location as the Certgen script, which holds the list of servers (IDM, CAFÉ, WEB, and manager service), in short names (without domain) for which certificates are to be created.
- Once you execute the script, the output will be a CSR and private key files.

Step 2: Upload the CSR file to a certificate authority (in our case it's Microsoft CA). The result of step 2 will be a certificate and root/chain files.

Step 3: Input the private key (step 1) and the root and certificate (step 2) files to the Certgen script to create the PEM and PFX certificate formats.

Step 4: The combination of certificates in PEM format and the private key file will be used in the CAFÉ and Identify management appliance.

Step 5: The certificates in PFX format will be used the IaaS Web and manager service component.

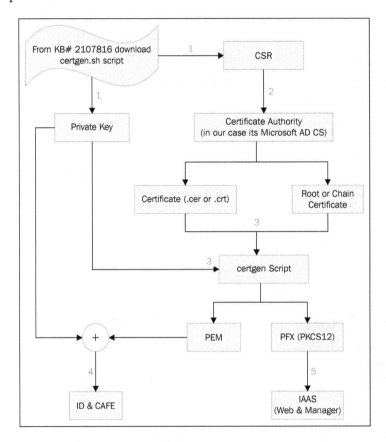

Now that we recognize the steps involved in creating the certificates, let's get started!!!

Instructions on how to install and configure Microsoft Certificate Authority are out of the scope of this book. However, you can refer to `https://blogs.vmware.com/consulting/2014/05/vcloud-automation-center-6-certificates-z.html` for the steps. If you are using Windows 2012 Server, refer to `http://www.careexchange.in/how-to-install-certificate-authority-on-windows-server-2012/` for instructions. Check out `http://kb.vmware.com/kb/2106583` for details on the supported hash algorithm. Ensure that you follow the instructions in *Creating vRA certificate templates* and *Adding a new template to certificate templates* to set up certificate template in this chapter.

Creating vRA certificate templates

To allow export of the certificate key, you need to create a non-standard certificate template that is a modified copy of the standard web server template. In addition, the Microsoft CA will be updated to allow for **Subject Alternative Names (SANs)** as specified in the attributes:

1. Connect to the root CA server or subordinate CA server.

2. Go to **Start** | **Run**, type `certtmpl.msc`, and click on **OK**. The Certificate Template Console opens.

3. In the middle pane, under **Template Display Name**, locate **Web Server**.

4. Right-click on **Web Server** and click on **Duplicate Template**.

5. In the **Duplicate Template** window, select **Windows Server 2003** for backward compatibility.

6. Click on the **General** tab.

7. In the **Template Display Name** field, enter `vRA_Certificate` as the name of the new template.

8. Click on the **Extensions** tab:

    1. Select **Key Usage** and click on **Edit**.

    2. Then select the **Signature is proof of origin (nonrepudiation)** option.

    3. Select the **Allow encryption of user data** option.

    4. Click on **OK**.

    5. Select **Application Policies** and click on **Edit**.

    6. Next, click on **Add**.

7. Select **Client Authentication**.

8. Click on **OK**.

9. Click on **OK** again.

9. Click on the **Subject Name** tab:

    1. Ensure that the **Supply in the request** option is selected.

10. Click on the **Request Handling** tab.

    1. Ensure that the **Allow private key to be exported** option is selected.

    2. Click on **OK** to save the template.

Adding a new template to certificate templates

Connect to the root CA server or subordinate CA server. Then follow these steps:

 Connect to the CA server in which you intend to perform your certificate generation.

1. Go to **Start | Run**, type `certsrv.msc`, and click on **OK**. The **Certificate Server** console opens.

2. In the left pane, if collapsed, expand the node by clicking on the **+** icon.

3. Right-click on **Certificate Templates** and go to **New | Certificate Template to Issue**.

4. Locate **vRA_Certificate** under the **Name** column.

5. Click on **OK**.

Creating certificates

I cannot stress more on how important it is for us to get this step correct. Otherwise, you will end up spending an awful lot of time troubleshooting the installation or configuration failure. That said, let's pay undivided attention as we move forward:

1. Since we have decided to go with the IDM appliance (clarification on the design approach is elucidated later in this chapter), we download the Certgen script on the IDM appliance. Create a file called `servers.txt` and add the list of servers for which certificates need to be created, as shown here:

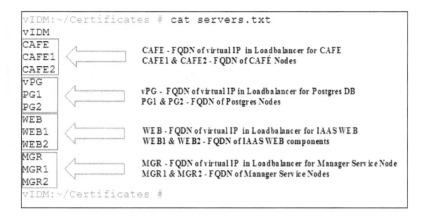

2. Execute the `chmod 755 certgen.sh` command to make the script executable. Then execute the Certgen script (`vIDM: ~ /Certificates # ./certgen.sh`) and follow the on-screen instructions:

```
Enter Organization:
PACKT

Enter Organizational Unit:
Publication

Enter Locality/Town:
BNG

Enter State/County:
KA

Enter Country Code (2 lettered ISO code e.g. GB,US,etc):
IN

Found server list file, containing the following names:
vIDM
CAFE
CAFE1
CAFE2
vPG
PG1            List of servers from server.txt file
PG2
WEB
WEB1
WEB2
MGR
MGR1
MGR2



Do you wish to import the servers from this file? (y/n):
y

Enter domain name to be used for non fully qualified hostnames (e.g. mycompany.com):
HINT: Press enter to add short hostnames to certificate exactly as listed above i.e. without appending any domain
PKCT.LOCAL
```

Once you enter the domain, the script will present you with the certificate request information on the screen. You can either copy and paste the information in the Certificate Authority web page to generate the certificate, *or* press *Ctrl + C* to stop the script execution. I would prefer to choose the latter.

The following screenshot shows the list of files created after executing the Certgen script for the first time:

```
vIDM:~/Certificates # ls -lhtr
total 40K
-rwxr--r-- 1 root root  16K Oct  2 13:12 certgen.sh
-rw------- 1 root root   75 Oct  2 22:01 servers.txt
-rw------- 1 root root 1.7K Oct  2 22:37 vrealize.key  ━━━━━ Private Key
-rw------- 1 root root 1.5K Oct  2 22:37 vrealize.csr  ━━━━━ Certificate Signing Request
-rw------- 1 root root 1.7K Oct  2 22:37 vrealize-orig.key
-rw------- 1 root root  192 Oct  2 22:37 vrealize-certs.log
-rw------- 1 root root  984 Oct  2 22:37 config.cfg
vIDM:~/Certificates #
```

3. Copy the CSR and private key files to the CA server to generate the certificate:

   1. Log in to the Microsoft CA web interface. The default link is `http://CA_server_FQDN/CertSrv`.

   2. Click on the **Request a certificate** link.

   3. Then click on **Advanced certificate request**.

   4. Click on the **Submit a certificate request by using a base-64-encoded CMC or PKCS #10 file, or submit a renewal request by using a base-64-encoded PKCS #7 file** link.

   5. Open the CSR file (`vrealize.csr`) in a text editor and copy the portion from -----BEGIN CERTIFICATE REQUEST---- to -----END CERTIFICATE REQUEST----- into the **Saved Request** box.

 Ensure that there are no new lines after -------END CERTIFICATE REQUEST------.

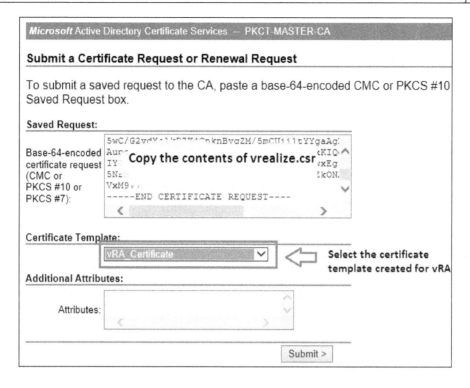

6. Click on **Submit**.

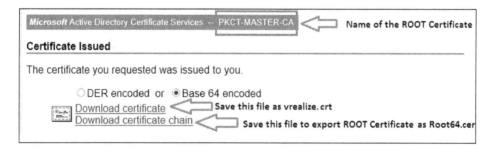

7. Right-click and open the saved file (`certnew`) in Crypto Shell extensions and exporting the root file as `Root64.cer`. Remember to select the **Base-64 encoded X.509 (.CER)** format.

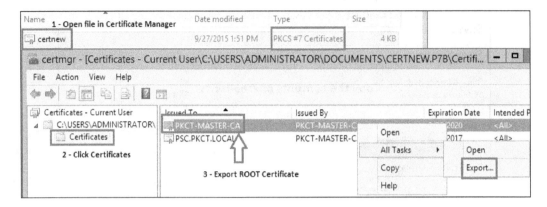

4. Continue the execution of the Certgen script once `Root64.cer` and `vrealize.crt` are stored in the Certgen script location.

```
vIDM:~/Certificates # ls -lstr
total 44
16 -rwxr--r-- 1 root root 15510 Oct  2 13:12 certgen.sh
 4 -rw------- 1 root root    75 Oct  2 22:01 servers.txt
 4 -rw------- 1 root root  1679 Oct  2 22:37 vrealize.key
 4 -rw------- 1 root root  1533 Oct  2 22:37 vrealize.csr
 4 -rw------- 1 root root  1679 Oct  2 22:37 vrealize-orig.key
 4 -rw------- 1 root root   984 Oct  2 22:37 config.cfg
 4 -rw------- 1 root root  1262 Oct  2 23:18 Root64.cer  <== Script expects root file saves as Root64.cer
 4 -rw------- 1 root root  2470 Oct  2 23:26 vrealize.crt <== Script expects certificate to be saved
vIDM:~/Certificates #                                       as vrealize.crt
```

5. Start the script execution again and follow the on-screen instructions, as shown here:

```
vIDM:~/Certificates # ./certgen.sh
*****************************************************
*      VMware vRealize - Signed Certificate Tool      *
*         CSE Reference Architecture Team             *
*****************************************************
Existing certificate request found in /root/Certificates. Use this request? (y/n)
y
Save your signed certificate as vrealize.crt in /root/Certificates and hit Enter:

Download your Root CA Certificate and save it as Root64.cer in /root/Certificates and hit Enter. Optionally, you can exit this script here and
 resume later:

Please create a PFX file password (store this safely as this will be used when importing accross components)
Enter Password:
```

 The password used is changeme.

Once the script finishes successfully, it will load the screen with instructions on how to upload the certificates for every ID appliance, CAFÉ, IaaS, application services, vRO, and vROPS products. The following screenshot is pertinent to the products in our installation:

```
Private Key for vRealize Automation (vCAC) and Identity Appliance
----------------------------------------------------------------
File: /root/Certificates/vrealize.key
Installation Method:
Go to https://vcac-server:5480 and paste into the Private Key box on the SSL page
Notes: Passphrase is the PFX password you entered earlier

PEM without Private Key for vRealize Automation (vCAC) and Identity Appliance
----------------------------------------------------------------------------
File: /root/Certificates/vrealize.pem
Installation Method:
Go to https://vcac-server:5480 and paste into the Certificate Chain box on the SSL page
Notes: Passphrase is the PFX password you entered earlier

PFX for vRealize Automation IAAS - IIS
--------------------------------------
File: /root/Certificates/vrealize.pfx
Installation Method:
Copy file to all IAAS servers
Double click the vrealize.pfx file
Click Next until the wizard finishes, accepting default options
```

Take a look at the next screenshot and check out the list of files generated after executing the script for the second time:

```
vIDM:~/Certificates # ls -lhtr
total 100K
-rwxr--r-- 1 root root  16K Oct  2 13:12 certgen.sh
-rw------- 1 root root   75 Oct  2 22:01 servers.txt
-rw------- 1 root root 1.7K Oct  2 22:37 vrealize.key ———— Private Key for CAFE and ID Appliance
-rw------- 1 root root 1.5K Oct  2 22:37 vrealize.csr
-rw------- 1 root root 1.7K Oct  2 22:37 vrealize-orig.key
-rw------- 1 root root  984 Oct  2 22:37 config.cfg
-rw------- 1 root root 1.3K Oct  2 23:18 Root64.cer ———— Root Certificate
-rw------- 1 root root 2.5K Oct  2 23:26 vrealize.crt
-rw------- 1 root root 4.3K Oct  2 23:29 vrealize.pfx ———— Certificate for IAAS Web & Manager Components
-rw------- 1 root root 4.0K Oct  2 23:29 vrealize.pem ———— PEM Encoded certificate for CAFE and ID Appliance
-rw------- 1 root root   16 Oct  2 23:29 vrealize-certs.log
-rw------- 1 root root 4.3K Oct  2 23:29 ssoserver.p12
-rw------- 1 root root 5.3K Oct  2 23:29 vrealize-full.pem ———— PEM Encoded certificate for vROPS
-rw------- 1 root root 4.7K Oct  2 23:29 server.xml.bak
-rw------- 1 root root 4.7K Oct  2 23:29 server.xml
-rw------- 1 root root 3.9K Oct  2 23:29 jssecacerts ———— JKS Certificate Store for vRO
-rw------- 1 root root 3.9K Oct  2 23:29 appdui.jks
vIDM:~/Certificates #
```

This concludes the steps involved in generating the certificate. Let's proceed to install and configure the ID appliance.

Identity management for authentication and authorization by vRA components

This is one of the critical components used by vRealize automation for authentication and authorization. Since we chose to use the NSX load balancer service in our design, our preference was to go with the ID appliance from the list of supported options at the time of writing this book. Let's comprehend the argument behind our choice:

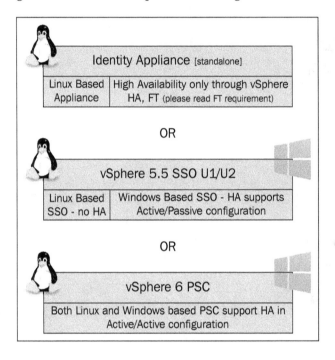

The identity (ID) appliance

The major benefit of running the vRealize identity appliance is that it is released as part of the vRealize Automation product. This is important because if new features are released in vRealize Automation that have dependencies on specific support from the SSO server, the identity appliance will be updated with the needed support. This will allow you to upgrade when a new version is released without having to worry about external dependencies.

It is recommended that the ID appliance be used in small deployments (10,000 managed machines and 500 catalog items).

The high availability option is possible only through VMware FT and HA. Starting from vSphere 6, since FT supports a maximum of four vCPUs, we can scale up the resources (CPU/memory) for the ID appliance if we see increased resource utilization:

vSphere 5.5 U1/U2 SSO

° The vCenter SSO server is the single point of administration for your SSO infrastructure. It's not a huge benefit, but in large environments, it can make an impact.

° vRealize Automation and vCenter are on two different release cycles.

° If you need to perform maintenance that requires you to bring down the SSO server, users will not be able to access vRealize Automation during that maintenance window.

° A Windows-based SSO component can be installed separately, and HA options are possible using the NSX load balancer.

° The NSX load balancer provides support for Windows-based SSO; it's an active-passive configuration (manual failover).

° Linux-based SSO is included in the **vCenter Appliance** (**VCVA**); high availability cannot be achieved individually for SSO. However, planning for vCenter will take care of SSO as well.

vSphere 6.0 PSC

° Starting from vSphere 6.0, SSO is named PSC and it is installed as a separate virtual appliance for both Linux and Windows versions.

° High availability can be achieved exclusively for PSC (both versions) using a load balancer, but NSX does not provide support yet (other load balancers such as F5 and NetScaler do provide support). So, using PSC is ruled out since the NSX load balancer cannot be used at the time of writing this book.

Identity appliance configuration

In this section, we will walk you through the step-by-step procedure of configuring the identity appliance. It is mandatory that we take care of the prerequisites to successfully complete the configuration.

Prerequisites

1. Allocate the hostname and IP address and create the DNS records (A and PTR) for the ID appliance.

2. Power on the ID virtual appliance once it's deployed (*I'm not going to walk through OVA deployment in this book*).

3. Connect to the VAMI page of the virtual appliance at `https://<IP-address-or-FQDN-of-ID-appliance|:5480`.

4. Navigate to **Network | Address**:

    ◦ Check whether the hostname and DNS entries are accurate

    ◦ The IP settings should be set to static

5. Navigate to **Admin | Admin** and check whether SSH is enabled and **Status** shows **Running**.

6. Navigate to **Admin | Time Settings** and ensure that the NTP settings are pointing to your infrastructure NTP server.

7. SSH into the virtual appliance as root user, and check whether you are able to ping the infrastructure management virtual machines (AD and DNS) using FQDN.

If all of this is true, move on to the next step.

Configuration

Once we are confident that the registered prerequisites are taken care of, we will institute the configuration:

1. The first step towards configuration is to initialize SSO. Go to the **SSO** tab, key in the password of your choice, and click on **Apply**. Wait until **SSO Status** reports **RUNNING**, like this:

2. Navigate to the **Host Settings** tab and confirm that the hostname has been populated, as follows:

3. Navigate to the SSL tab and select **Import PEM encoded Certificate**. Copy the contents of `vrealize.key` into the **RSA Private Key** section and the contents of `vrealize.pem` into the **Certificate Chain** section. Use the same passphrase that was used at the time of creating the certificates.

4. This will be the last step before we conclude the configuration of the ID appliance. Navigate to the **Active Directory** tab and join it to the domain in your infrastructure, like this:

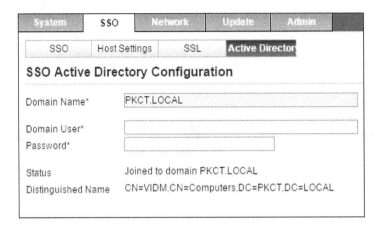

NSX load balancer configuration

Assuming that NSX Manager and NSX Edge are already deployed as parts of the infrastructure, we will focus our efforts on NSX load balancer configuration for the CAFÉ appliance, the Postgres database, IaaS Web, and the manager service.

Prerequisite

During the initial setup process, the load balancer might tend to route half of the traffic to the secondary node, which is not yet installed and will result in an installation failure. To avoid such failures, we need to perform the following tasks:

- The health/service monitor settings will vary before and after the installation of every component. Read the load balancer configuration for every component as you progress and make the recommended changes.

- Disable all secondary nodes from the load balancer pools when you begin the installation of the first node.

Configuring the external vPostgres DB in HA for the vRealize Automation CAFÉ appliance

It is recommended that you use an external instance of the vPostgres database for the CAFÉ appliance in a high availability (HA) environment. However, since the release of VMware vRealize Automation standalone, VMware vFabric Postgres is the end of availability and is no longer available as a standalone product. To address customers' needs, VMware developed a way to utilize the database instance located in the VMware vRealize Automation appliance in HA mode without having to incur additional licensing.

The following steps are clearly documented at `http://kb.vmware.com/kb/2108923`. We will follow exactly the same steps given here, with some screenshots for ease of understanding.

Prerequisites

Allocate the hostname and IP address, and create DNS records (A and PTR) for the virtual IP of the vPostgres DB and two vPostgres DB nodes:

1. Create the NSX load balancer configurations for the vPostgres database.

2. Freshly deploy two VMware vRealize Automation 6.2 appliances without any configurations (*I'm not going to walk through OVA deployment in this book*).

3. Before powering them on, add a 20 GB disk to both the appliances (for better performance, add the eager zero thick disk type).

4. Power on and perform the following checks in both the appliances.

5. Connect to the VAMI page of the virtual appliance: `https://<IP_address-or_FQDN-of-ID-appliance|:5480`.

6. Navigate to **Network | Address**:

    ° Check whether the *hostname* and *DNS* entries are accurate.

    ° The IP settings should be set to static.

7. Navigate to **Admin- | Admin**. Check whether SSH is enabled and **Status** shows **Running**.

8. Navigate to **Admin-** | **Time Settings** and ensure that the NTP settings are pointing to your infrastructure NTP server.

9. Perform SSH into the virtual appliance as root user, and check whether you are able to ping the virtual IP of the vPostgres database in the load balancer and the infrastructure management virtual machines (AD and DNS) using FQDN.

If all the preceding parameters are true, proceed to the next step.

Setup details

The following details will be used for our setup:

FQDN	Hostnames	IP address	Purpose
PG.PKCT.LOCAL	vPG	10.0.0.111	FQDN for the virtual IP in the NSX load balancer
PG1.PKCT.LOCAL	PG1	10.0.0.112	First vPostgres DB node for the CAFÉ appliance
PG2.PKCT.LOCAL	PG2	10.0.0.113	Replication vPostgres DB node for the CAFÉ appliance

vPostgres NSX load balancer configurations

This section only describes the load balancing aspect of the NSX product configuration, assuming that NSX has already been configured and validated to work properly on the target environment or networks:

1. Log in to vCenter Server where NSX has been configured.

2. Navigate to **Home** | **Networking & Security** | **NSX Edges** and select the **Edge appliance** deployed for the use of the distributed vRealize Automation installation.

3. Navigate to **Manage** | **Settings** and select the **Interfaces** menu on the left-hand side.

4. Select the first vNIC and click on the **Edit** button.

5. This will be your load balancer virtual appliance.

6. Click on the **Add** button to assign a static IP address (virtual IP for vPostgres) to the virtual interface.

7. Once completed, navigate to the load balancer tab.

Application Profile configuration

This configuration will not change throughout the setup:

Name	Type	Enable SSL pass-through	Persistence
Postgres	TCP	Leave it unchecked	None

Service Monitoring configuration

Pre-installation: The configuration will change after the installation of Postgres DB

Name	Interval	Timeout	Retries	Type	Method	URL	Receive
Postgres_SM	5	10	3	TCP	N/A	N/A	N/A

Pool configuration

Pre-installation: We will be adding the details of the secondary node post installation

Pool name	Algorithm	Monitors	Member name	Example IP address	Port	Monitor Port
Postgres_ Pool	IP_HASH	Postgres_ SM	PG1	10.0.0.112	5432	5480

Virtual Server configuration

This configuration will not change throughout the setup:

Application profile	Name	IP address	Protocol	Port	Default pool
Postgres	Postgres_TCP	10.0.0.111	TCP	5432	Postgres_Pool

vPostgres configuration

Download and copy the 2108923_dbCluster.zip file attached to
http://kb.vmware.com/kb/2108923 to both the appliances.

> VMware KB# 2108923 has detailed instructions on how to configure
> replication between two vPostgres databases that will be used in the
> CAFÉ appliance. All the relevant instructions will be followed to
> achieve replication between databases.

Connect to the appliance (PG1 and PG2) via SSH and extract the `tar xvf 2108923_dbCluster.tar` files:

1. Execute the command in *both* the appliances: `./configureDisk.sh /dev/sdd`:

```
PG1:~/2108923_dbCluster # ./configureDisk.sh /dev/sdd
1.) Validating /dev/sdd exists
/dev/sdd found
2.) Creating partition: /dev/sdd1
Information: You may need to update /etc/fstab.

   Towards the end look for WAL message

Ownership changed successfully
WAL Archive disk configured successfully
PG1:~/2108923_dbCluster #

━━━━━━━━━━━━━━━━━━━━━━━━

PG2:~/2108923_dbCluster # ./configureDisk.sh /dev/sdd
1.) Validating /dev/sdd exists
/dev/sdd found
2.) Creating partition: /dev/sdd1
Information: You may need to update /etc/fstab.

   Towards the end look for WAL message

Ownership changed successfully
WAL Archive disk configured successfully
PG2:~/2108923_dbCluster #
```

2. Then execute this command in *both* the appliances:

```
./pgClusterSetup.sh -d vPG.PKCT.LOCAL -w changeme -r changeme -p
changeme
```

> vPG.PKCT.LOCAL - FQDN of virtual IP for vPostgres in NSX Load balancer

> changeme - This password can be anything of users choice

```
./pgClusterSetup.sh [-d] db_fqdn [-w] db_pass [-r] replication_
password [-p] postgres_password
```

> [-d] Database load balancer fully qualified domain name

> [-w] Database password (will set password to this value)

> [-r] Replication password (Optional: will use Database password if not set)

> [-p] Postgres password (Optional: will use Database password if not set)

This command prepares the appliance database for clustering:

```
PG1:~/2108923_dbCluster # ./pgClusterSetup.sh -d vPG.PKCT.LOCAL -w changeme -r changeme -p changeme
***********************************************************************
*     VMware vRealize Automation Center - vPostgres Clustering Setup      *
***********************************************************************

    Wait until you see "Finished" after step 11

Finished
PG1:~/2108923_dbCluster #


PG2:~/2108923_dbCluster # ./pgClusterSetup.sh -d vPG.PKCT.LOCAL -w changeme -r changeme -p changeme
***********************************************************************
*     VMware vRealize Automation Center - vPostgres Clustering Setup      *
***********************************************************************

    Wait until you see "Finished" after step 11

Finished
PG2:~/2108923_dbCluster #


vPG.PKCT.LOCAL - FQDN for virtual IP of vPostgres in the NSX Loadbalancer || changeme - this password can be anything of your choice

    ./pgClusterSetup.sh [-d]  db_fqdn  [-w]  db_pass  [-r]  replication_password  [-p]  postgres_password
    [-d] Database load balancer fully qualified domain name
    [-w] Database password (will set password to this value)
    [-r] Replication password (Optional: will use Database password if not set)
    [-p] Postgres password (Optional: will use Database password if not set)
```

3. Configure database replication:

    ° In this setup, PG1 will serve as the master and PG2 will act as the slave (replica) node.

    ° Perform SSH into PG2 and execute the following command:

    ```
    PG2:~ # su - postgres

    Last login: Mon Oct  5 11:28:31 UTC 2015 on pts/0

    postgres@PG2:~| /opt/vmware/vpostgres/current/share/run_as_
    replica  -h  PG1.PKCT.LOCAL  -b  -W  -U  replicate
    ```

Enter the replicate users password when prompted (the password is changeme).

Type yes after verifying the thumbprint of the primary machine.

Enter the Postgres users password (it is changeme).

Type yes when prompted with **Type yes to enable WAL archiving on primary**.

Then type yes when prompted with **WARNING: the base backup operation will replace the current contents of the data directory. Please confirm by typing yes:**.

4. To check the status of the replication, execute this command from both master (PG1) and slave (PG2):

> The command related to the database should be executed using a postgres user. To switch a user from root to postgres, execute this command:
>
> **su - postgres**

- ° Navigate to the /opt/vmware/vpostgres/current/share path
- ° Executing show_replication_status from master should list the slave node, as follows:

If you want to perform a test failover, read http://kb.vmware.com/kb/2108923 for instructions.

Testing Replication

Here is an easy and quick way to check whether the replication works before we move on to the next step:

1. Create a test table in the master (PG1) node and check whether it is replicated in the slave (PG2) node, like this:

```
    Login to Master
PG1:~ # su - postgres   Switching user from root to postgres
Last login: Mon Oct  5 12:00:44 UTC 2015 on pts/0
postgres@PG1:~> /opt/vmware/vpostgres/current/bin/psql   Logging into postgres shell
psql.bin (9.2.10)
Type "help" for help.

postgres=# CREATE TABLE test_replication(test varchar(20));   Creating Table
CREATE TABLE
postgres=# INSERT INTO test_replication VALUES ('data for replication');
INSERT 0 1                       Insert values into table
postgres=#

    Login to Slave and check if test_replication table is streamed/replicated

PG2:~ # su - postgres
Last login: Mon Oct  5 11:48:39 UTC 2015 on pts/0
postgres@PG2:~> /opt/vmware/vpostgres/current/bin/psql
psql.bin (9.2.10)
Type "help" for help.

postgres=# SELECT * FROM test_replication;   Checking if table is replicated
          test
---------------------
 data for replication
(1 row)

postgres=#
```

2. Drop the table from the Master (PG1) node, as shown in the following screenshot:

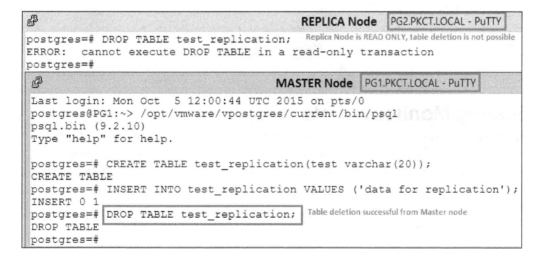

Postgres Monitor scripts

This section provides information on a set of scripts that are to be used in conjunction with a load balancer to direct traffic to the master (writeable) appliance database instance.

Configuration

While connected to the Postgres nodes using SSH, log out the `postgres` user from both master and slave nodes.

Go to `http://kb.vmware.com/kb/2127052`, download the monitor scripts, and upload them to both the Postgres (CAFÉ) appliances. Extract the files using the `tar xvf 2127052-monitor-script.tar.gz` command.

Now follow the instructions in the screenshot given here in both the appliances (`PG1` and `PG2`):

```
PG1:~/2108923_dbCluster # chmod 755 vPostgresNodeState.py vPostgresService.py
PG1:~/2108923_dbCluster # cp vPostgresNodeState.py vPostgresService.py /opt/vmware/share/htdocs/
PG1:~/2108923_dbCluster # cd /opt/vmware/share/htdocs
PG1:/opt/vmware/share/htdocs # touch postgresNodes.txt
PG1:/opt/vmware/share/htdocs # chmod 755 postgresNodes.txt
PG1:/opt/vmware/share/htdocs #


PG2:~/2108923_dbCluster # chmod 755 vPostgresNodeState.py vPostgresService.py
PG2:~/2108923_dbCluster # ls -lhtr
total 20K
-rwxr-xr-x 1 root root 8.3K May 20 21:11 vPostgresService.py
-rwxr-xr-x 1 root root 5.1K May 20 21:11 vPostgresNodeState.py
PG2:~/2108923_dbCluster # cp vPostgresNodeState.py vPostgresService.py /opt/vmware/share/htdocs/
PG2:~/2108923_dbCluster # cd /opt/vmware/share/htdocs/
PG2:/opt/vmware/share/htdocs # touch postgresNodes.txt
PG2:/opt/vmware/share/htdocs # chmod 755 postgresNodes.txt
PG2:/opt/vmware/share/htdocs #
```

Testing Monitor scripts

From the browser, connect to the FQDN of the Postgres appliance (*not the load balancer FQDN*). Depending on which node is the master or the slave, a response (`true` or `false`) is received, as shown in the next screenshot. The `PG1` node is the master in our configuration.

Only if you receive a response, as shown in this screenshot, should you move on to the next step:

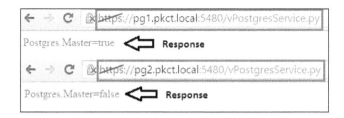

Updating the NSX load balancer configuration for vPostgres

Since the vPostgres database configuration is complete, we need to update the initial NSX load balancer settings (service monitoring and pool) for vPostgres.

Service monitoring configuration

Update the existing configuration to reflect the following changes:

Name	Interval	Timeout	Retries	Type	Method	URL	Receive
Postgres_SM	5	10	3	HTTPS	GET	/vPostgres Service.py	Postgres. Master=true

Pool configuration

Update the existing configuration to reflect these changes:

Pool name	Algorithm	Monitors	Member name	Example IP	Port	Monitor port
Postgres_Pool	IP_HASH	Postgres_SM	PG1	10.0.0.112	5432	5480
			PG2	10.0.0.113	5432	5480

You may add the entries of the second node (PG2), but ensure that you uncheck **Enable Member** in the pools configuration. Since the Postgres database cluster runs in active-standby mode, the second database node (standby) cannot accept any SQL transaction. Moreover, in the event of a database failure, manual failover is required. The bottom line: always disable the standby database node.

So, the key to a successful Postgres configuration is to ensure that your pool status is set to UP after this configuration. If not, troubleshoot and fix this before proceeding.

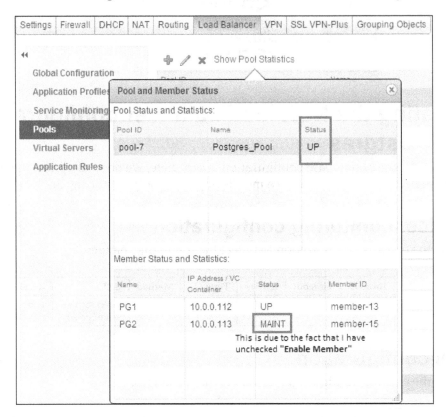

Configuring the CAFÉ appliance in HA

Now that we have completed the installation of the vPostgres database and identity appliance, let's start the installation of the CAFÉ appliance. In this section, let's look at the recipe of configuring two CAFÉ nodes in cluster mode.

Prerequisites

Allocate the hostname and IP address, and create DNS records (A and PTR) for the CAFÉ virtual IP in the load balancer and two CAFÉ nodes (CAFE1 and CAFE2):

1. Create NSX load balancer configurations for CAFÉ.

2. Freshly deploy two VMware vRealize Automation 6.2 appliances without any configurations (again, *I'm not going to walk through OVA deployment in this book*).

3. Power on and perform the following checks in both the CAFÉ appliances:

    ° Connect to the VAMI page of the virtual appliance: `https://<IP_address-or_FQDN-of-CAFE(1/2)-appliance|:5480`.

    ° Navigate to **Network | Address**.

      Check whether the *hostname* and *DNS* entries are accurate.

      The IP settings should be set to *static*.

    ° Navigate to **Admin- | Admin,** and check whether SSH is enabled and **Status** shows **Running**.

    ° Navigate to **Admin | Time Settings** and ensure that the NTP settings are pointing to your infrastructure NTP server.

    ° Perform SSH into the virtual appliance as root user, and check whether you are able to ping the virtual IP of CAFÉ in the load balancer and the infrastructure management virtual machines (AD and DNS) using FQDN.

    ° Take a memory snapshot of both the CAFÉ nodes using the web client or C# client.

    ° If all the preceding parameters are true in both the appliances, proceed to the next step.

> Before starting the configuration of the CAFÉ appliance, take a memory snapshot of both the Postgres database nodes. Since details about the CAFÉ nodes will be stored in the database, it is easy to roll back both the CAFÉ and the Postgres database if any errors are encountered while configuring the cluster.

Setup Details

The following details will be used for our setup:

FQDN	Hostnames	IP address	Purpose
CAFE.PKCT.LOCAL	CAFE	10.0.0.114	FQDN for virtual IP in the NSX load balancer
CAFE1.PKCT.LOCAL	CAFE 1	10.0.0.115	The first CAFÉ node
CAFE 2.PKCT.LOCAL	CAFE 2	10.0.0.116	The second CAFÉ node

CAFÉ NSX load balancer configurations

This section only describes the load balancing aspect of NSX product configuration, assuming that NSX has already been configured and validated to work properly on the target environment or networks:

1. Log in to vCenter Server where NSX has been configured.

2. Navigate to **Home | Networking & Security | NSX Edges,** and select the **Edge appliance** deployed for the use of the distributed vRealize Automation installation.

3. Navigate to **Manage | Settings** and select the **Interfaces** menu on the left-hand side.

4. Select the first vNIC and click on the **Edit** button.

5. This will be your load balancer virtual appliance.

6. Click on the **Add** button to assign a static IP address (virtual IP for CAFE) to the virtual interface.

7. Once completed, navigate to the load balancer tab.

Application Profile configuration

This configuration will not change throughout the setup:

Name	Type	Enable SSL passthrough	Persistence
CAFE	HTTPS	Checked	None

Service Monitoring configuration

Initial configuration: Configuration will be updated after CAFÉ node's installation and configuration

Name	Interval	Timeout	Retries	Type	Method	URL	Receive
CAFÉ_SM	5	10	3	TCP	N/A	N/A	N/A

Pool configuration

Initial configuration:

Pool name	Algorithm	Monitors	Member name	Example IP address	Port	Monitor Port
CAFÉ_WEB_POOL	IP_HASH	CAFÉ_SM	CAFE1	10.0.0.115	443	443
CAFÉ_Console_POOL	IP_HASH	CAFÉ_SM	CAFE1	10.0.0.115	8444	443

Virtual servers configuration

This configuration will not change throughout the setup:

Application profile	Name	IP address	Protocol	Port	Default pool
CAFE	CAFÉ_WEB	10.0.0.114	HTTPS	443	CAFÉ_WEB_POOL
CAFE	CAFÉ_CONSOLE	10.0.0.114	HTTPS	8444	CAFÉ_Console_POOL

CAFÉ configuration

In this section, we will configure the cluster between the CAFE1 and CAFE2 nodes for high availability. In vRA 6.1, this option was called **HA**, but in vRA 6.2, it is called **Cluster**. If you recollect, the CAFÉ has an active-active HA configuration with automatic failover:

1. Log in to the CAFE1 VAMI portal as a root user (https://CAFE1.PKCT. LOCAL:5480).

2. Navigate to **vRA Settings | Host Settings** and fill in the details as shown in the next screenshot after next step.

3. Please note that we are importing the certificates that were created earlier. Click on **Save Settings** to enable the configurations:

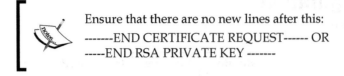

Ensure that there are no new lines after this:
-------END CERTIFICATE REQUEST------ OR
-----END RSA PRIVATE KEY -------

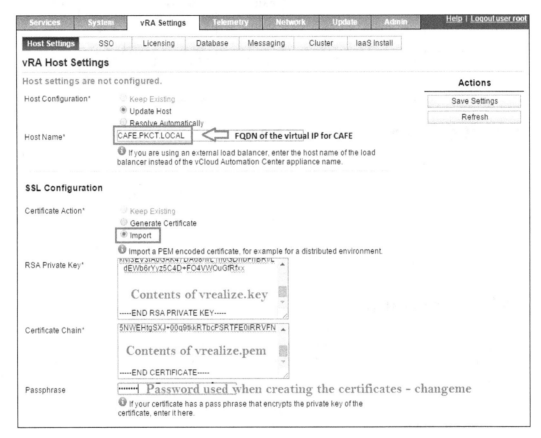

4. Once the **Host Settings** configuration is complete, *do not change* the resulting configuration, as shown here:

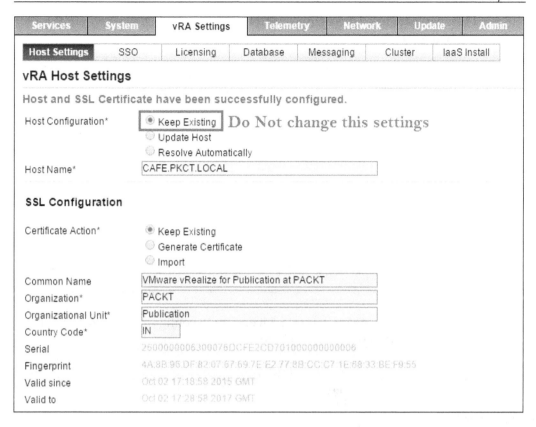

5. Navigate to **vRA Settings | Database** to configure persistent storage for the CAFÉ appliance, as shown in the screenshot:

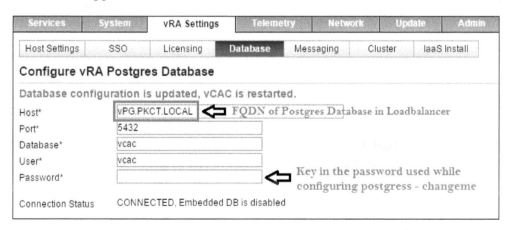

6. Then navigate to **vRA Settings | SSO** to configure SSO, as shown in the following screenshot:

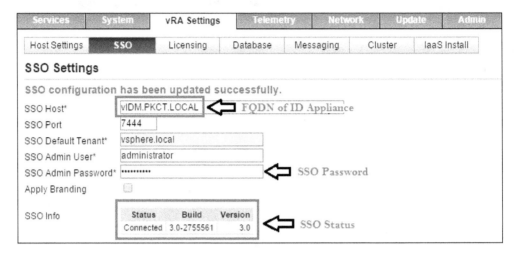

7. Next, navigate to **vRA Settings | Licensing** to configure the licensing. This will conclude the configuration in the CAFE1 appliance.

8. Cluster configuration:

   ° Log in to the second CAFE VAMI portal as a root user (https://CAFE2.PKCT.LOCAL:5480).

○ Navigate to **vRA Settings | Cluster** and fill in the details as per this screenshot:

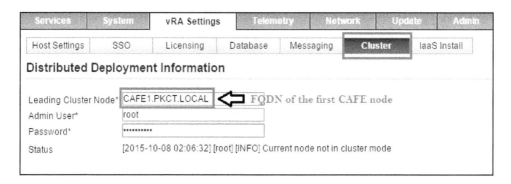

○ Once the cluster configuration is complete, the `vcac-server` service will be restarted.

○ Navigate to the **Services** tab in the VAMI page, and wait until all the services are in the **REGISTERED** state in both the CAFÉ nodes. Wait for at least 20 minutes before making changes to the NSX load balancer for CAFÉ.

Updating the NSX load balancer configuration for CAFÉ

Once the CAFÉ cluster configuration is complete, the pools and service monitoring settings in the load balancer should be updated for failover to work.

Service Monitoring configuration

Update the existing configuration to reflect the following changes (once all the 27 services have *started in both the appliances*):

Name	Interval	Timeout	Retries	Type	Method	URL	Receive
CAFÉ_SM	5	10	3	HTTPS	GET	/vcac/ services/ api/status	REGISTERED

Pools configuration

Update the existing configuration to reflect these changes:

Pool name	Algorithm	Monitors	Member name	IP address	Port	Monitor port
CAFÉ_WEB_POOL	IP_HASH	CAFÉ_SM	CAFE1	10.0.0.115	443	443
			CAFE2	10.0.0.116	443	443
CAFÉ_Console_POOL	IP_HASH	CAFÉ_SM	CAFE1	10.0.0.115	8444	443
			CAFE2	10.0.0.116	8444	443

Once the preceding settings are complete, check whether the CAFÉ nodes are in the **UP** status in **Show Pool Statistic** under **Pools** in the NSX load balancer:

We need to perform one last step before the CAFÉ configuration can be deemed as complete. Open a web browser and connect to the CAFÉ service monitoring URL: `https://CAFE.PKCT.LOCAL/vcac/services/api/status`. Check whether you see **REGISTERED** for the **shell-ui-app** service, as shown in the following screenshot:

IaaS installation

Infrastructure as a Service (IaaS) enables the rapid modeling and provisioning of servers and desktops across virtual and physical, private and public, or hybrid cloud infrastructures. Access to the infrastructure features is provided by the IaaS component. The installation of all IaaS components takes place on a Windows machine (physical or virtual).

The IaaS component of vRealize Automation includes multiple parts:

- MS SQL database
- IaaS Web Server
- IaaS Manager Service
- Distributed Execution Managers (Orchestrator and Workers)
- Proxy Agents

A list of supported OSes and databases for installing IaaS components can be found at https://www.vmware.com/pdf/vrealize-automation-62-support-matrix.pdf.

The following configuration will be used in this setup:

- All IaaS components will be installed in a virtual machine
- Windows OS—Windows 2012 Standard
- Database—SQL Server 2008 R2 RTM (10.50.1600.1) Enterprise Edition (x64)

The following are just recommendations for virtual machine configuration; feel free to make changes as per your requirement:

Component (per VM)	vCPU	vRAM	Storage
Model Manager Web	2	4	40
Manager Service + Orchestrator	4	4	40
DEM Worker + Proxy Agent	4	6	40

 Make sure you log in as a domain administrator or create a service account (domain user) to run the downloaded installer, and *it's extremely important to set the password to never expire since all the services installed by IaaS component will run under this account.*

IaaS components HA modes and failover options

Let's look at the different HA and failover modes available for each IaaS component. They are shown here:

IaaS Components	HA Mode	Failover Mode	
Web Server	Active - Active	Automatic	
Manager Server	Active - Passive	Manual	Will be installed in the same Node
DEM Orchestrator	Active - Passive	Manual	
DEM Worker	Active - Active	Automatic	Will be installed in the same Node
Proxy Agents	Active - Active	Automatic	

IaaS prerequisites and virtual machine preparation

Keep this flowchart as a reference to prepare all the virtual machines before installing the IaaS component.

Alternatively, you may choose to perform the following steps in a single virtual machine, convert it into a template, and deploy from the template using vCenter customization. Personally, I would not prefer this since I faced issues while configuring MSDTC:

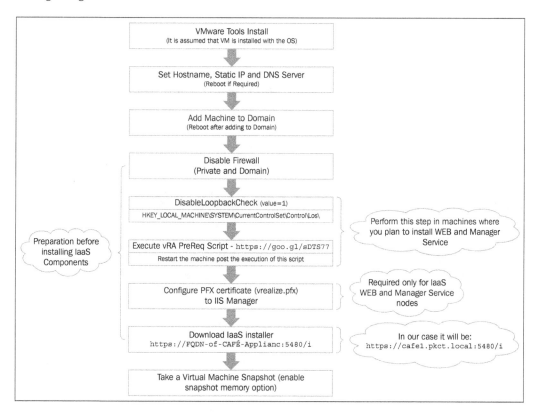

Overview of the IaaS installation flow (only the first nodes)

In this chapter, we will install the first node for all the IaaS components and perform a functional test to affirm that the installation thus far is upright. Based on the results, we will proceed to install the second nodes for high availability in the distributed architecture. I created the below flow chart which typically illustrates the installation process.

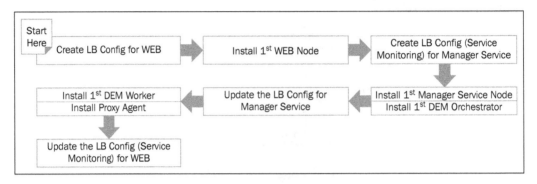

Installing PFX certificate to IIS Web Server

Uploading the PFX certificate to the IIS web server is a requirement since IaaS components (Model Manager WEB and Manager Service) use the IIS web server during installation. In this example, the WEB2 node is used. The following are the steps for installing a PFX certificate on the IIS web server:

1. Log in to the Node (WEB or MGR) before starting the installation as a Domain Administrator or service account user with sufficient privileges.

2. Go to **Server Manager** | **Tools** | **IIS Manager** and select **WEB2** (if you have logged in to the **WEB1** node, you will see **WEB1 (user account)**). Then click on **Server Certificates** under **IIS**:

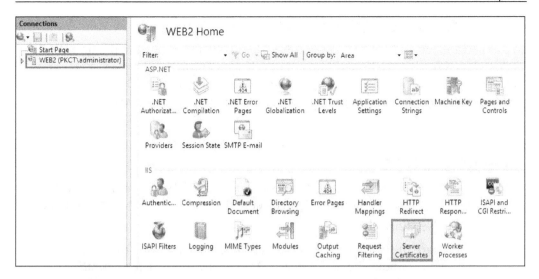

3. Towards the top-right corner, click on **Import** under **Actions**. Load the certificate and enter the password used at the time of creating the certificate. Select the **Personal** certificate store and click on **OK**. Make sure you select the **Allow this certificate to be exported** option, as shown here:

Installation of the First Web node

In this section, we will take at a look at how to install and configure the first WEB node, which is called the Model Manager Web, also known as Repository. It exposes the IaaS data model as a service and allows CRUD operations on the IaaS database. It also implements the business logic that is executed by **Distributed Execution Manager (DEM)**.

Prerequisites

- Allocate the hostname and IP address, and create DNS records (A and PTR) for the WEB virtual IP in the load balancer and two WEB nodes (WEB1 and WEB2)

- Create NSX load balancer configurations for WEB

- To prepare the virtual machine for IaaS node installation, follow the instructions under the *IaaS prerequisites and virtual machine preparation* topic in this chapter

- To install the IIS certificates, follow the instructions under the *Installing PFX certificate to IIS web server* topic in this chapter

Setup details

The following details will be used for our setup:

FQDN	Hostnames	IP address	Purpose
WEB.PKCT.LOCAL	WEB	10.0.0.117	FQDN for virtual IP in NSX load balancer
WEB1.PKCT.LOCAL	WEB 1	10.0.0.118	First WEB node
WEB 2.PKCT.LOCAL	WEB 2	10.0.0.119	Second WEB node

NSX load balancer configurations for IaaS web

This section only describes the configuration in NSX Manager. It is assumed that NSX setup has already been configured and validated to work properly in the target environment or networks

1. Log in to vCenter Server where NSX has been configured.

2. Navigate to **Home** | **Networking & Security** | **NSX Edges** and select the **Edge appliance** deployed for the use of the distributed vRealize Automation installation.

3. Navigate to **Manage** | **Settings** and select the **Interfaces** menu on the left-hand side.

4. Select the first vNIC and click on the **Edit** button.

5. This will be your load balancer virtual appliance.

6. Click on the **Add** button to assign a static IP address (a virtual IP for IaaS WEB) to the virtual interface.

7. Once completed, navigate to the load balancer tab.

Application Profile configuration

This configuration will not change throughout the setup:

Name	Type	Enable SSL pass-through	Persistence
WEB	HTTPS	Checked	None

Service Monitoring configuration

Pre-installation: The configuration will be updated later

Name	Interval	Timeout	Retries	Type	Method	URL	Receive
WEB_SM	5	10	3	ICMP	N/A	N/A	N/A

Pool configuration

Pre-installation: The secondary WEB nodes details will be added later

Pool name	Algorithm	Monitors	Member name	IP address	Port	Monitor port
WEB_Pool	IP_HASH	WEB_SM	WEB1	10.0.0.118	443	443

Virtual Server configuration

This configuration will not change throughout the setup:

Application profile	Name	IP address	Protocol	Port	Default pool
WEB	IAAS_WEB	10.0.0.117	HTTPS	443	WEB_Pool

Make sure that the pool status for WEB is **UP**. Otherwise, the installation will never succeed. This is possible only if you set **Service Monitoring** to **ICMP**.

Once the WEB1 node installation is successful, proceed to install Manager Service and Orchestrator in the same machine without changing the NSX LB configuration for WEB.

Checkpoint

Before starting the IaaS server installation, navigate to the IIS Manager and highlight **Default Web Site**:

1. Click on **Bindings...** and then on **Add...**, like this:

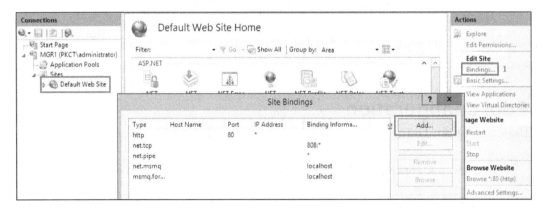

2. Select **Type** as **https** and ensure that you load the certificate (manually imported as part of the prerequisites) from the drop-down menu under **SSL certificate**, as shown in the following screenshot. Click on **OK**:

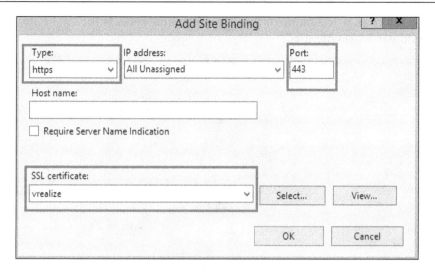

3. Open the web browser and type the FQDN of the IaaS web virtual IP in load balancer: `https://WEB.PKCT.LOCAL`. You will be prompted for the credentials of the `WEB1` machine since the load balancer will be redirecting the request to the available pool member (`WEB1`). If the default IIS Microsoft web page opens up after entering the credentials, it means the prevalidation is successful.

4. Proceed to remove the `https` binding by clicking on **Remove** and go to the next step (do not skip this step).

IaaS WEB installation

In this section, we will take a look at how to install and configure the first WEB node, which is called the Model Manager Web, also known as *repository* node:

1. Log in to the `WEB1` machine using the domain user or service account user created for the installation:

2. Connect to one of the CAFÉ nodes and download the IaaS installer from `https://CAFE1.PKCT.LOCAL:5480/i`

3. Do not change the name of this file—the name reflects the CAFÉ node from where it is downloaded:

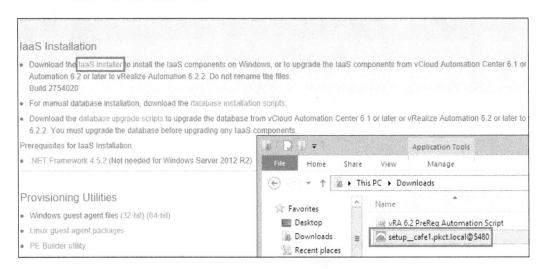

4. Right-click on the downloaded file and select **Run as Administrator** to begin installation.

5. Enter the credentials for the CAFÉ1 appliance, check **Accept Certificate** as shown in the following screenshot, and click on **Next**:

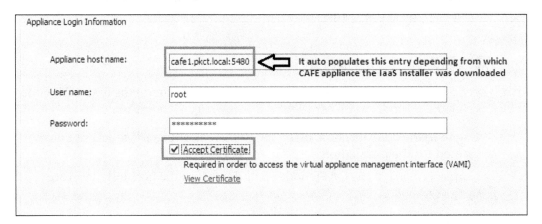

6. Select **Custom Install** and then choose **IaaS Server** in **Component Selection**.

7. Database configuration:

Ensure that MSDTC is enabled in the Database Machine used by IaaS components (DO NOT SKIP):

Go to **Control Panel | Administrative Tools | Component Services**.

Expand **Component Services | Computers | My Computer | Distributed Transaction Coordinator**.

Right-click on **Local DTC** and click on **Properties**. Then click on the **Security** tab.

Select the **Network DTC Access** option.

Next, select the **Allow Remote Client** and **Allow Remote Administration** options.

Select the **Allow Inbound** and **Allow Outbound** options as well.

Specify NetworkService for DTC Log in Account.

Click on **OK**.

8. Configuration of the Web UI:

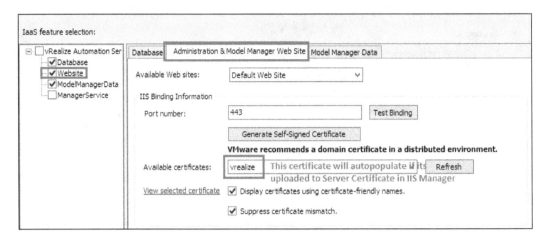

9. Configuration of the **Model Manager Data**:

    ◦   Enter the FQDN of the CAFÉ virtual IP in load balancer.

    ◦   Click on **Load** to populate the SSO tenant.

    ◦   Click on **Download** to populate the certificate information for the SSO tenant.

    ◦   Fill in the other details as shown in the following screenshot and click on **Next**:

[Click on **Test** to validate that the connection is successful.]

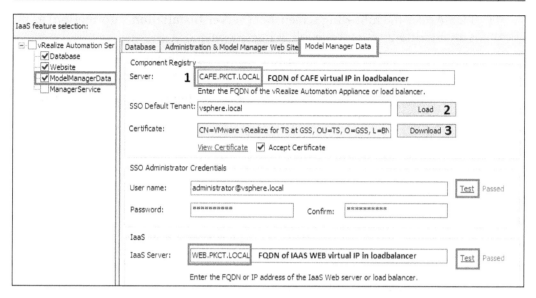

10. The installer will execute the Prerequisite checker; if every requirement is satisfied, the **Bypass** button will be grayed out. Click on **Next** to proceed.

 Even if a single or a simple requirement is not met, the installer will allow you to proceed with the installation by enabling the Bypass option. Do not take this route, as it is recommended that every requirement be satisfied.

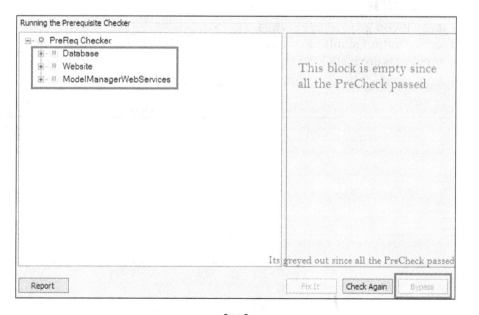

11. Please refer the following screenshot (**Server Installation Information**) as it is an important step for the following reasons:

   ○ The username will be used by all services installed by the product. This is why we recommended setting the password to never expire.

   ○ Passphrase — Read the text in the following screenshot which has the detailed explanation:

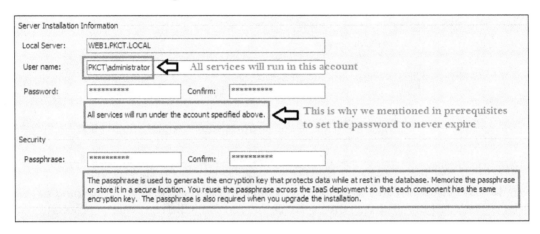

12. Click on **Install** to start the installation of the product. Once the installation is successful, continue with the configuration of the Manager Service.

Checkpoint

At this stage, if you go to `https://WEB.PKCT.LOCAL/WAPI/api/status`, you should see the output similar to the next screenshot. This is expected since no DEM components are installed yet:

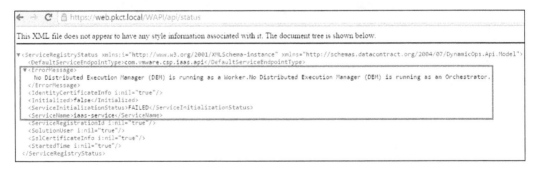

Installation of the first Manager Service and DEM Orchestrator node

In this section, we will walk you through the step-by-step recipe of installing the Manager Service and DEM Orchestrator component in a single server since both follow identical HA failover behavior. However, Manager Service requires a manual failover while the DEM Orchestrator is automatic.

Prerequisites

The prerequisites for installing the first manager service and DEM orchestrator node are as follows:

- Allocate the hostname and IP address, and create DNS records (A and PTR) for the WEB virtual IP in load balancer and two MGR nodes (MGR1 and MGR2).

- Create NSX load balancer configurations for MGR.

- To prepare the virtual machine for IaaS node installation, follow the instructions under the *IaaS prerequisites and virtual machine preparation* topic in this chapter.

- To install the IIS certificates, follow the instructions under the *Installing PFX certificate to IIS web server* topic in this chapter.

Setup Details

The following details will be used for our setup:

FQDN	Hostnames	IP address	Purpose
MGR.PKCT.LOCAL	MGR	10.0.0.120	FQDN for virtual IP in NSX load balancer
MGR1.PKCT.LOCAL	MGR1	10.0.0.121	First MGR node
MGR2.PKCT.LOCAL	MGR2	10.0.0.122	Second MGR node

NSX load balancer configurations for IaaS MGR

This section only describes the load balancing aspect of the NSX product configuration, assuming that NSX has already been configured and validated to work properly on the target environment or networks:

1. Log in to vCenter Server where NSX has been configured.
2. Navigate to **Home | Networking & Security | NSX Edges** and select the **Edge appliance** deployed for the use of distributed vRealize Automation installation.
3. Navigate to **Manage | Settings** and select the **Interfaces** menu on the left-hand side.
4. Select the first vNIC and click on the **Edit** button.
5. This will be your load balancer virtual appliance.
6. Click on the **Add** button to assign a static IP address (virtual IP for the Manager Service) to the virtual interface.
7. Once completed, navigate to the load balancer tab.

Application Profile configuration

This configuration will not change throughout the setup:

Name	Type	Enable SSL passthrough	Persistence
MGR	HTTPS	Checked	None

Service Monitoring configuration

Pre-installation: This configuration will be updated later

Name	Interval	Timeout	Retries	Type	Method	URL	Receive
MGR_SM	5	10	3	TCP	N/A	N/A	N/A

Pool configuration

Pre-installation:

Pool name	Algorithm	Monitors	Member name	IP address	Port	Monitor port
MGR_Pool	IP_HASH	MGR_SM	MGR1	10.0.0.121	443	443

Virtual Server configuration

This configuration will not change throughout the setup:

Application profile	Name	IP address	Protocol	Port	Default pool
MGR	IAAS_MGR	10.0.0.120	HTTPS	443	MGR_Pool

 Note that it is normal to see the pool status for MGR node in **DOWN** state before installation.

IaaS MGR and Orchestrator Installation (first/active node)

Both the Manager Service and DEM Orchestrator will be installed in the same node since they have similar HA and failover modes. Log in to the MGR1 virtual machine and perform steps 1 to 3 while installing the first IaaS WEB node:

1. Since this will be the active node, select **Active node with startup type set to automatic**, as shown in the following screenshot, and click on **Next**:

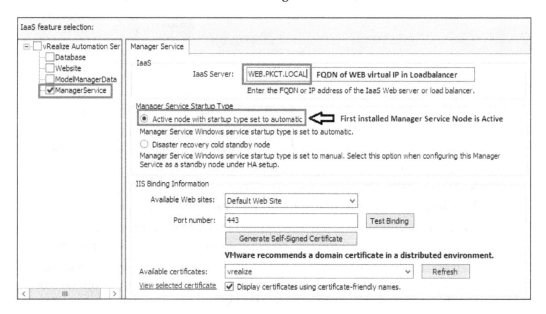

2. The installer will execute the Prerequisite checker; if every requirement is satisfied, the **Bypass** button will be greyed out. Click on **Next** to proceed.

3. Even if a single or a simple requirement is not met, the installer will allow you to proceed with the installation by enabling the **Bypass** option. Do not take this route as it is recommended that you satisfy every requirement.

4. Update all of the required information on the server installation page, as follows:

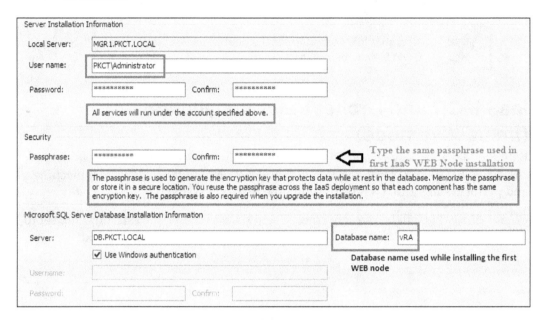

5. Click on **Install** to start the installation of the product. Once the installation is successful, we will proceed to install DEM Orchestrator in the same node.

6. Use the same installer (`setup_cafe1.pkct.local@5480`) to install DEM Orchestrator on the `MGR1` node. Right-click on the installer and select **Run as Administrator** to begin the installation.

7. On the installation type page, select **Custom Install** and then choose **Distributed Execution Managers** under **Component Selection**.

8. The installer will execute the Prerequisite checker; if every requirement is satisfied, the **Bypass** button will be grayed out. Click on **Next** to proceed.

9. Even if a single or a simple requirement is not met, the installer will allow you to proceed with the installation by enabling the **Bypass** option. Do not take this route, as it is recommended that you satisfy every requirement.

10. Type in the credentials for the user account used for installation, and click on **Next**.

11. Select **Orchestrator** in the **DEM role**.

12. Type the **DEM name** of your choice. For this setup, we will use the name **DEM-O**.

13. After entering the FQDN of the load balancer virtual IP for the Manager Service, click on **Test** to validate that the nodes are reachable.

14. Click on **Add** to register the Orchestrator role.

15. Click on **Next** and then click on **Install** on the next screen to begin the installation:

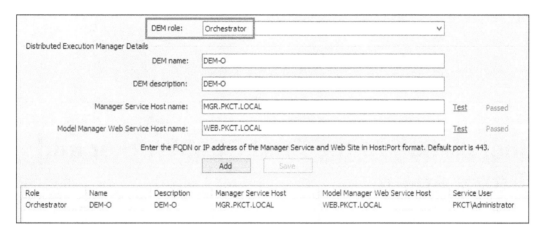

Checkpoint

Open the web browser and type this URL: `https://MGR.PKCT.LOCAL/VMPS2`. If the installation of the Manager Service is intact, you should see the `Receive` string `BasicHttpBinding_VMPSProxyAgent_policy` (refer to the following screenshot). If the output matches what is shown in the screenshot (except for the node names), go ahead to install the DEM Worker and proxy agent:

```xml
<?xml version="1.0" encoding="UTF-8"?>
<wsdl:definitions xmlns:soapenc="http://schemas.xmlsoap.org/soap/encoding/"
xmlns:wsaw="http://www.w3.org/2006/05/addressing/wsdl" xmlns:soap="http://schemas.xmlsoap.org/wsdl/soap/"
xmlns:tns="http://tempuri.org/" xmlns:xsd="http://www.w3.org/2001/XMLSchema"
xmlns:wsam="http://www.w3.org/2007/05/addressing/metadata"
xmlns:wsa="http://schemas.xmlsoap.org/ws/2004/08/addressing" xmlns:soap12="http://schemas.xmlsoap.org/wsdl/soap12/"
xmlns:msc="http://schemas.microsoft.com/ws/2005/12/wsdl/contract"
xmlns:wsap="http://schemas.xmlsoap.org/ws/2004/08/addressing/policy"
xmlns:wsp="http://schemas.xmlsoap.org/ws/2004/09/policy" xmlns:wsa10="http://www.w3.org/2005/08/addressing"
xmlns:wsu="http://docs.oasis-open.org/wss/2004/01/oasis-200401-wss-wssecurity-utility-1.0.xsd"
xmlns:i0="http://microsoft.com/VMPS" xmlns:wsx="http://schemas.xmlsoap.org/ws/2004/09/mex"
xmlns:wsdl="http://schemas.xmlsoap.org/wsdl/" targetNamespace="http://tempuri.org/" name="GuestAgentWorkItemService">
  + <wsp:Policy wsu:Id="BasicHttpBinding_VMPSProxyAgent_policy">
    <wsdl:import location="https://mgr1.pkct.local/VMPS2?wsdl=wsdl0" namespace="http://microsoft.com/VMPS"/>
    <wsdl:types/>
  + <wsdl:binding name="BasicHttpBinding_VMPSProxyAgent" type="i0:VMPSProxyAgent">
  + <wsdl:service name="GuestAgentWorkItemService">
</wsdl:definitions>
```

Updating the **Service Monitoring** setting for MGR and WEB in load balancer is not mandatory at this stage. If you go to `https://WEB.PKCT.LOCAL/WAPI/api/status`, you will see a response similar to the screenshot here. The error message is expected since we are yet to install DEM Worker.

```
← → C   🔒 https://web.pkct.local/WAPI/api/status

This XML file does not appear to have any style information associated with it. The document tree is shown below.

▼<ServiceRegistryStatus xmlns:i="http://www.w3.org/2001/XMLSchema-instance" xmlns="http://schemas.datacontract.org/2004/07/DynamicOps.Api.Model">
    <DefaultServiceEndpointType>com.vmware.csp.iaas.api</DefaultServiceEndpointType>
  ▼<ErrorMessage>
      No Distributed Execution Manager (DEM) is running as a Worker.
    </ErrorMessage>
    <IdentityCertificateInfo i:nil="true"/>
    <Initialized>false</Initialized>
    <ServiceInitializationStatus>FAILED</ServiceInitializationStatus>
    <ServiceName>iaas-service</ServiceName>
    <ServiceRegistrationId i:nil="true"/>
    <SolutionUser i:nil="true"/>
    <SslCertificateInfo i:nil="true"/>
    <StartedTime i:nil="true"/>
  </ServiceRegistryStatus>
```

Installation of the First DEM Worker and Proxy Agent

In this section, we will show you the step-by-step way to install the first DEM Worker and proxy agent on a single server.

Prerequisites

- Allocate the hostname and IP address, and create DNS records (A and PTR) for the Worker node.

- Follow the instructions from the *IaaS prerequisites and virtual machine preparation* section in this chapter.

- Since we will not execute the vRA PreReq PowerShell script in this node, we have to ensure that we take care of these three requirements:

  - Install .NET 4.5.2

  - Enable MSDTC (refer to page 30)

  - Start the **Secondary Logon Service** from `services.msc` until the installation is complete

Setup Details

The following details will be used for our setup:

FQDN	Hostnames	IP address	Purpose
WRK1.PKCT.LOCAL	WRK1	10.0.0.124	FQDN for first worker node
WRK2.PKCT.LOCAL	WRK2	10.0.0.125	FQDN for second worker node

Worker installation

Log in to the WRK1 node as the domain user or the service account user created for installation, and perform steps 1 and 2 while installing the IaaS WEB node:

1. On the installation type page, select **Custom Install** and then choose **Distributed Execution Managers** under **Component Selection**.

2. The installer will execute the Prerequisite checker; if every requirement is satisfied, the **Bypass** button will be grayed out. Click on **Next** to proceed.

3. Once again, even if a single or a simple requirement is not met, the installer will allow you to proceed with the installation by enabling the **Bypass** option. Do not take this route, as it is recommended that you satisfy every requirement.

4. Provide the credentials for the server installation page:

    1. Select **Worker** in the **DEM role**.

    2. Type a **DEM name** of your choice.

    3. After entering the FQDN of the load balancer virtual IP for the Manager Service and Web nodes, click on **Test**.

    4. Click on **Add** to register the DEM role.

5. Click on **Next**, and then click on **Install** on the next screen to begin the installation:

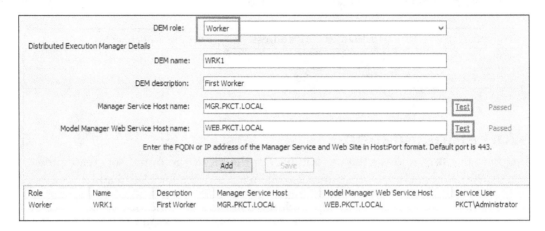

Once the installation of DEM Worker is complete, start the installation of the proxy agent.

Proxy Agent installation

A proxy agent is a type of infrastructure agent used to interact with hypervisor endpoints for the provisioning of virtual machines. vRA has the ability to have multiple vCenters as endpoints. This is cool if you need to do true multi-tenancy and a tenant has security requirements that require them to have their own vCenter instance. There can be multiple proxy agents pointing to the same endpoint for high availability reasons.

In order to include an additional vCenter Server in vRA, you'll need to install an additional agent; every vCenter instance requires its own agent:

1. Right-click on the installer (`setup_cafe1.pkct.local@5480`) used to install DEM Worker and select **Run as Administrator** to begin the installation.

2. On the installation type page, select **Custom Install** and then choose **Proxy Agents** under **Component Selection**.

3. Once again, the installer will execute the Prerequisite checker; if every requirement is satisfied, the **Bypass** button will be grayed out. Click on **Next** to proceed.

4. Even if a single or a simple requirement is not met, the installer will allow you to proceed with the installation by enabling the **Bypass** option. Do not take this route, as it is recommended that you satisfy every requirement.

5. Select the **Agent type** as **vSphere**.

6. Type the **Agent name**. (Note: A Windows service will be created with this name post the installation of the proxy agent)

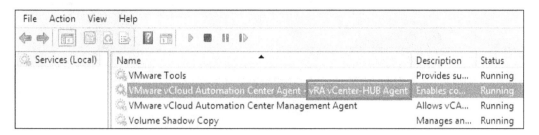

7. After entering the FQDN of the load balancer virtual IP for the manager service and Web nodes, click on **Test**.

8. Enter the **Endpoint** name. You'll use this name as the endpoint name when adding the vCenter to vRA — they *must* match.

9. Click on **Add** to register the vSphere Agent type.

10. Click on **Next**, and then click on **Install** on the next screen to begin the installation:

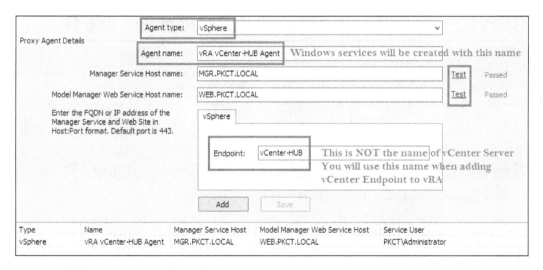

Once the installation of the proxy agent is complete, open a browser and connect to this URL: `https://WEB.PKCT.LOCAL /WAPI/api/status`.

If the installation of all IaaS components is intact, you should receive a response similar to this screenshot:

This XML file does not appear to have any style information associated with it. The document tree is shown below.

```
▼<ServiceRegistryStatus xmlns:i="http://www.w3.org/2001/XMLSchema-instance" xmlns="http://schemas.datacontract.org/2004/07/DynamicOps.Api.Model">
    <DefaultServiceEndpointType>com.vmware.csp.iaas.api</DefaultServiceEndpointType>
    <ErrorMessage i:nil="true"/>
    <IdentityCertificateInfo i:nil="true"/>
    <Initialized>true</Initialized>
    <ServiceInitializationStatus>REGISTERED</ServiceInitializationStatus>
    <ServiceName>iaas-service</ServiceName>
    <ServiceRegistrationId i:nil="true"/>
    <SolutionUser i:nil="true"/>
    <SslCertificateInfo i:nil="true"/>
    <StartedTime i:nil="true"/>
</ServiceRegistryStatus>
```

Only if the output matches what is shown in the screenshot, proceed to update the **Service Monitoring** setting for both WEB and MGR in the load balancer.

Updating the NSX load balancer configuration for WEB and MGR

Here are the final configuration setting for WEB and MGR nodes.

Service monitoring configuration for WEB

Update the existing configuration to reflect the following changes:

Name	Interval	Timeout	Retries	Type	Method	URL	Receive
WEB_SM	5	10	3	HTTPS	GET	/WAPI/api/ status	iaas-service

Service monitoring configuration for MGR

Update the existing configuration to reflect these changes:

Name	Interval	Timeout	Retries	Type	Method	URL	Receive
MGR_SM	5	10	3	HTTPS	GET	/VMPS2	BasicHttpBinding_ VMPSProxyAgent_ policy

This concludes the installation of the first node for IaaS components.

Summary

Based on my experience, the most challenging part is the first half of the installation in distributed vRealize Automation, where the configuration of all the components should be performed in a sequence.

While documentation around configuration exists helter-skelter on the Web, the sequence is definitely non-existent.

This chapter has covered all the salient configuration steps in a sequence for every component. I am definitely confident that if you follow each step in this chapter, the first half of the installation should be a cakewalk.

Upon completing the first half of the installation, a functional test is compulsory to endorse the outcome of the installation. The functional test will be performed in the beginning of the next chapter, followed by the installation of the secondary nodes for the IaaS component, consequently concluding the setup.

I would also encourage you to take a look at the VMware documentation for details about the different deployment types at `http://www.vmware.com/files/pdf/products/vCloud/VMware-vCloud-Automation-Center-61-Reference-Architecture.pdf?ClickID=bf61mle6ng6ygkkngmzdknnsymugdq1ulgne`.

In order to reinforce that the installation is operational, we will perform a validation test of our setup in the next chapter. Once the validation is successful, we will proceed with the installation of the remaining IaaS nodes and complete the distributed architecture.

3

Functional Validation – Phase 1 and Installing Secondary Nodes

When I started writing this chapter, I developed a sense of relief since we have already accomplished the taxing part of the installation. In order to reinforce that the installation is operational, we will perform the validation test of our setup in this chapter with the following steps:

- Creating a tenant
- Adding tenant and infrastructure administrator users
- Adding licensing
- Checking the DEM status

Once the preceding validation test is successful, we will proceed with the installation of the remaining IaaS nodes and complete the distributed architecture. For a quick recap, in *Chapter 2, Distributed Installation Using Custom Certificates*, we installed and configured the identity management appliance, vPostgres DB, CAFÉ nodes (cluster), IaaS components (Web, Manager Service, DEM Orchestrator, DEM Worker, and proxy agents) that establishes the foundation for the vRealize Automation solution.

Validation test

At this stage, we have completed the installation of the required components for vRealize Automation. Before we proceed, let's demonstrate that the installation thus far has come along up to the mark. To this purpose, we will be onboarding a tenant and adding administrators to manage it. As a last step, we will check whether the DEM node is active and online. Let's take a look at how this is done:

1. Log in to the default tenant portal using the SSO administrator credentials (`administrator@vsphere.local`)—`https://CAFE.PKCT.LOCAL/vcac`

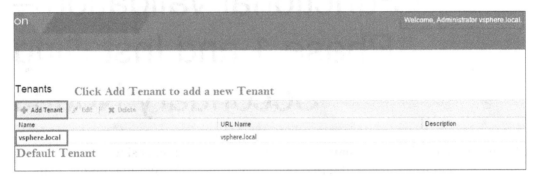

2. From the default page, click **Add Tenant** to create a new tenant *Publication* and then click **Submit** and **Next**:

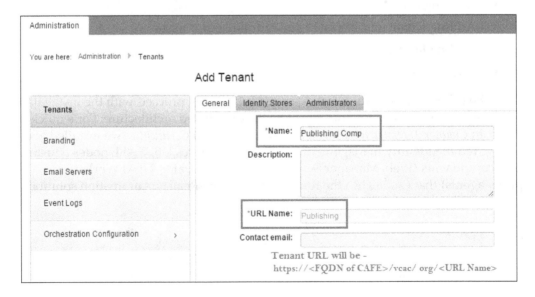

3. In the **Identity Stores** page, click **Add Identity Store** and fill in the required details and click **Add** to add the identity store. Click **Next** to proceed to the **Administrators** page:

4. Add the **Tenant administrators** and **Infrastructure administrators** users and click **Add** to finish the tenant creation process. You may choose to use the domain administrator for both the roles to avoid multiple logins and logouts while configuring the endpoints, blueprints, and service catalogs:

5. Log out the `administrator@vsphere.local` user from the default portal and log in to the `Publishing` tenant as infrastructure admin (`iadmin@pkct.local`)—`https://CAFÉ.PKCT.LOCAL/vcac/org/Publishing`:

> If the **Infrastructure** tab displays incorrect labels — reboot both the CAFÉ nodes followed by the WEB node to resolve this issue. Refer to *Failover of CAFÉ appliance* section in *Chapter 6, Testing Failover Scenarios for vRealize Automation Components* to make necessary changes to NSX load balancer before rebooting the CAFÉ appliance:

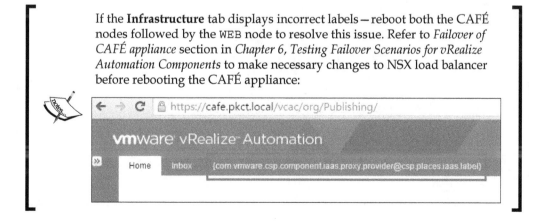

6. From the **Infrastructure** tab, navigate to **Administration | Licensing** and add the license keys.

7. Navigate to **Infrastructure | Monitoring | Distributed Execution Status**. You should see **Name** and **Status** of the DEM Orchestrator and Worker that were installed in *Chapter 2, Distributed Installation Using Custom Certificates*. Navigate to the other tabs and get familiarized with the portal:

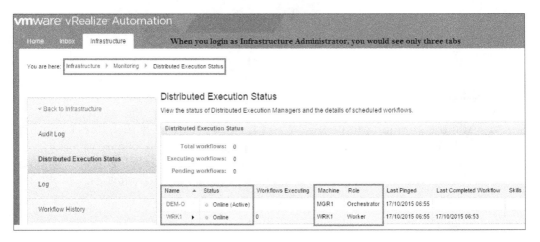

8. Log out the infrastructure admin and log in to `https://CAFÉ.PKCT.LOCAL/vcac/org/Publishing` as tenant administrator (`tadmin@pkct.local`) and navigate to all the tabs that are familiar with the portal:

If you have spent some quality time in the portal navigating all the tabs and options, let us advance to the next step by installing the secondary active/standby nodes in IaaS components.

Installing the second active web node

After successfully validating the setup, we will continue to install the secondary IaaS nodes.

Prerequisites

Here are the prerequisites for the installation:

- Update the *pools* configuration in the NSX load balancer for WEB server
    - Browse the health monitor URL of IaaS WEB server (https://WEB.PKCT.LOCAL/WAPI/api/status) and confirm if you receive REGISTERED response for service iaas-service

- To prepare the virtual machine for the IaaS node installation, follow the instructions from *Chapter 2, Distributed Installation Using Custom Certificates,* under the *IaaS prerequisites and virtual machine preparation* topic
- From *Chapter 2, Distributed Installation Using Custom Certificates,* follow the prerequisite instructions under *Installing PFX certificate to IIS web server*

NSX load balancer configurations for IaaS web

Update the existing pool configuration by adding the second WEB node; no other changes are required.

Pool configuration

Update the existing configuration to reflect the following changes:

Pool Name	Algorithm	Monitors	Member Name	IP Address	Port	Monitor Port
WEB_Pool	IP_HASH	WEB_SM	WEB1	10.112.103.114	443	443
			WEB2	10.112.103.115	443	443

Pools statistics after adding the second node

The pools status for the second node will be DOWN since the installation is yet to start:

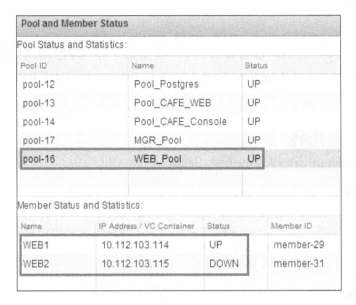

IaaS WEB installation (second node)

Now that we have completed the prerequisites for the secondary WEB node, let's proceed with the installation:

1. Log in to the WEB2 machine using the domain user or service account user created for the installation.

    ○ Connect to one of the CAFÉ nodes and download the IaaS installer—https://CAFE1.PKCT.LOCAL:5480/i

    ○ Do not change the name of this file—the name reflects the CAFÉ node from where it is downloaded

2. Right-click the downloaded file and select **Run as Administrator** to begin the installation.

    ○ Enter the credentials for the CAFÉ1 appliance and check **Accept Certificate** and click **Next**

3. Select **Custom Install** and then choose **IaaS Server** in **Component Selection**.

4. Configuration of website. After filling in the details, click **Test** to validate whether the connection is reachable and successful:

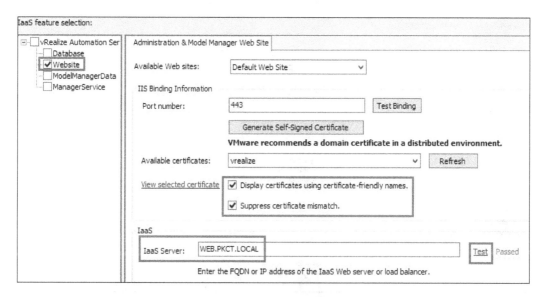

5. The installer will execute the prerequisite checker; if every requirement is satisfied, the **Bypass** button will be *grayed* out. Click **Next** to proceed.

    ○ Even if a single or a trivial requirement is not met, the installer will allow you to proceed with the installation by enabling the **Bypass** option. Do not take this route, as it is recommended to satisfy every requirement.

6. This is an important step for the following reasons:

    ○ The username will be used by all the services installed by the product. This is why we recommended to set the password to never expire.

○ **Passphrase** — the text in the screenshot has a detailed explanation:

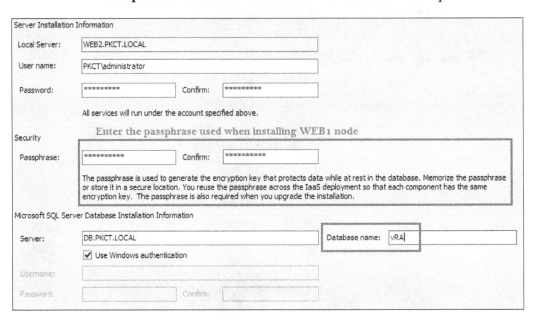

7. Click **Next** and then click **Install** to begin the installation. Once the installation is completed successfully, open a web browser and connect to the URL — `https://WEB2.PKCT.LOCAL/WAPI/api/status`; if the configuration is intact, you should receive a response similar to the following screenshot:

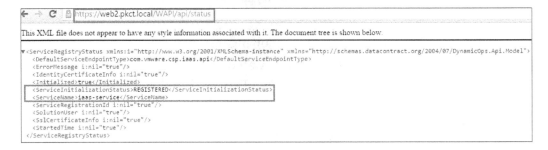

8. It is advisable to wait for at least 10 to 15 minutes before checking **Pools Statistics** in the NSX load balancer for the WEB configuration. Both the nodes should be in the UP status since the HA mode for Model Manager WEB is Active-Active:

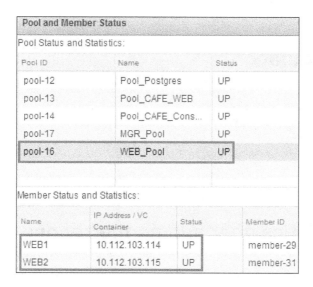

Installing the standby Manager Service and the DEM Orchestrator node

We will now see how to install the standby manager and DEM Orchestrator node.

Prerequisites

Here are the prerequisites for the installation:

- Update the pools configuration in NSX load balancer for MGR
    - Check if you receive the response BasicHttpBinding_ VMPSProxyAgent by accessing the health monitor page for Manager Service node – https://MGR.PKCT.LOCAL/VMPS2

- To prepare the virtual machine for IaaS node installation follow the instructions from *Chapter 2, Distributed Installation Using Custom Certificates* under *IaaS prerequisites and virtual machine preparation* topic

- From *Chapter 2, Distributed Installation Using Custom Certificates* follow the instructions under *Installing PFX certificate to IIS web server*

NSX load balancer configurations for IaaS MGR

Update the existing pool configuration by adding the second MGR node; no other changes are required.

Pool configuration

Update the existing configuration to reflect the following changes:

Pool Name	Algorithm	Monitors	Member Name	IP Address	Port	Monitor Port
MGR_ Pool	IP_HASH	MGR_SM	MGR1	10.112.103.117	443	443
			MGR2	10.112.103.118	443	443

Pools statistics after adding the second node

Since the HA mode for Manager Service is active-standby, all the additional node installed after the first node is considered *standby* and marks the node to DOWN status in the NSX load balancer.

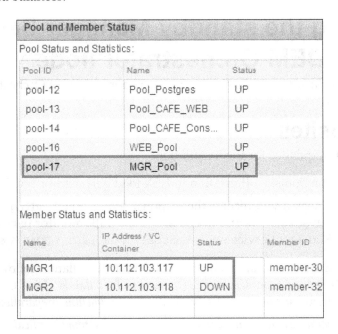

IaaS MGR and Orchestrator installation – (second/standby node)

Both Manager Service and DEM Orchestrator will be installed in the same node since they have a similar HA and failover modes.

1. Login to MGR2 virtual machine and perform steps 1 to 3 while installing the first or second IaaS WEB node.

2. Select **Disaster recovery cold standby mode** as the active node is already installed in *Chapter 2, Distributed Installation Using Custom Certificates* and click **Next**:

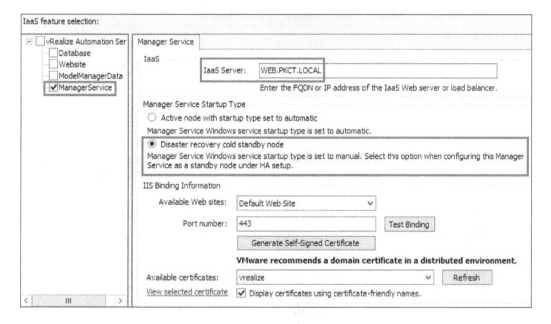

3. The installer will execute the prerequisite checker; if every requirement is satisfied, the **Bypass** button will be grayed out. Click **Next** to proceed.

    ° Even if a single or a trivial requirement is not met the installer will allow you to proceed with the installation by enabling the **Bypass** option. Do not take this route, as it is recommended to satisfy every requirement.

4. Update all the required information in the server installation page:

5. Click **Install** to start the installation of the product. Once the installation is successful, we will proceed to install the second DEM Orchestrator in the same node.

6. Use the installer (`setup_cafe1.pkct.local@5480`) to install DEM Orchestrator in the `MGR2` node. Right-click the installer and select **Run as Administrator** to begin installation.

7. In the **Installation Type** page, select **Custom Install** and then choose **Distributed Execution Managers** under **Component Selection**.

8. The installer will execute the prerequisite checker; if every requirement is satisfied, the **Bypass** button will be grayed out. Click **Next** to proceed.

   ° Even if a single or a trivial requirement is not met, the installer will allow you to proceed with the installation by enabling the **Bypass** option. Do not take this route, as it is recommended to satisfy every requirement.

9. Type in the credentials for the user account and click **Next**.

10. Select **Orchestrator** in **DEM role**.

   ◦ Type **DEM name** of your choice. For this setup, we will use the name, DEM-02.

   ◦ After entering the FQDN of the load balancer virtual IP for Manager Service, click **Test** to validate that the nodes are reachable.

   ◦ Click **Add** to register the Orchestrator role.

   ◦ Click **Next** and then click **Install** in the next screen to begin installation:

Checkpoint: Open the web browser and type https://MGR2.PKCT.LOCAL/VMPS2; since this node is installed as a standby node, you should get the response: **404 - File or directory not found**. However, if you go to https://MGR.PKCT.LOCAL/VMPS2, you should see the Receive string, BasicHttpBinding_VMPSProxyAgent_policy, (refer to the screenshot) as the load balancer redirects the request to the active Manager Service node (MGR1):

```
<?xml version="1.0" encoding="UTF-8"?>
<wsdl:definitions xmlns:soapenc="http://schemas.xmlsoap.org/soap/encoding/"
  xmlns:wsaw="http://www.w3.org/2006/05/addressing/wsdl" xmlns:soap="http://schemas.xmlsoap.org/wsdl/soap/"
  xmlns:tns="http://tempuri.org/" xmlns:xsd="http://www.w3.org/2001/XMLSchema"
  xmlns:wsam="http://www.w3.org/2007/05/addressing/metadata"
  xmlns:wsa="http://schemas.xmlsoap.org/ws/2004/08/addressing" xmlns:soap12="http://schemas.xmlsoap.org/wsdl/soap12/"
  xmlns:msc="http://schemas.microsoft.com/ws/2005/12/wsdl/contract"
  xmlns:wsap="http://schemas.xmlsoap.org/ws/2004/08/addressing/policy"
  xmlns:wsp="http://schemas.xmlsoap.org/ws/2004/09/policy" xmlns:wsa10="http://www.w3.org/2005/08/addressing"
  xmlns:wsu="http://docs.oasis-open.org/wss/2004/01/oasis-200401-wss-wssecurity-utility-1.0.xsd"
  xmlns:i0="http://microsoft.com/VMPS" xmlns:wsx="http://schemas.xmlsoap.org/ws/2004/09/mex"
  xmlns:wsdl="http://schemas.xmlsoap.org/wsdl/" targetNamespace="http://tempuri.org/" name="GuestAgentWorkItemService">
  + <wsp:Policy wsu:Id="BasicHttpBinding_VMPSProxyAgent_policy">
    <wsdl:import location="https://mgr1.pkct.local/VMPS2?wsdl=wsdl0" namespace="http://microsoft.com/VMPS"/>
    <wsdl:types/>
  + <wsdl:binding name="BasicHttpBinding_VMPSProxyAgent" type="i0:VMPSProxyAgent">
  + <wsdl:service name="GuestAgentWorkItemService">
</wsdl:definitions>
```

If the output matches the preceding screenshot (except for the node names), move ahead to install DEM Worker and proxy agent.

Installing the second DEM Worker and proxy agent

In this section, we will install and configure the second DEM Worker and proxy agent nodes.

Prerequisites

Here are the prerequisites for the installation:

- To prepare the virtual machine for IaaS node installation, follow the instructions from *Chapter 2*, *Distributed Installation Using Custom Certificates*, under the *IaaS prerequisites and virtual machine preparation* topic

- Since the vRA PreReq PowerShell script will not be executed, manually secure the following three requirements:
    - Install .NET 4.5.2
    - Enable MSDTC (Refer to the *IaaS WEB installation* topic in *Chapter 2*, *Distributed Installation Using Custom Certificates*)
    - Start the **Secondary Logon** service from `services.msc` until the installation is complete

Worker installation

Log in to the WRK2 node as the domain user or the service account user created for installation and perform steps 1 and 2 while installing the IaaS WEB node:

1. In the **Installation Type** page, select **Custom Install** and then choose **Distributed Execution Managers** under **Component Selection**.

2. The installer will execute the prerequisite checker; if every requirement is satisfied, the **Bypass** button will be grayed out. Click **Next** to proceed.
    - Even if a single or a trivial requirement is not met, the installer will allow you to proceed with the installation by enabling the **Bypass** option. Do not take this route, as it is recommended to satisfy every requirement.

3. Provide the credentials in the server installation page and click **Next**:

4. Select **Worker** in **DEM role**.

   ° Type **DEM name** of your choice. For this setup, we will use the name, WRK2.

   ° After entering the FQDN of the load balancer virtual IP for Manager Service and Web nodes, click **Test** to validate that the nodes are reachable.

   ° Click **Add** to register the DEM role.

   ° Click **Next** and then click **Install** in the next screen to begin installation:

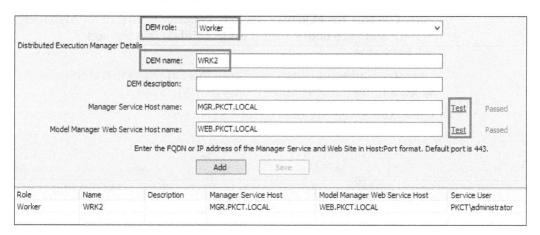

Once the installation of DEM Worker is complete, start the installation of the proxy agent.

Installing the proxy agent

As mentioned in *Chapter 2, Distributed Installation Using Custom Certificates*, multiple proxy agents can point to the same endpoint. We will be installing the second proxy agent for high availability reasons. Make sure that the endpoint name used in this installation matches with the first proxy agent name:

1. Use the installer (`setup_cafe1.pkct.local@5480`) used for installing DEM Worker. Right-click the installer and select **Run as Administrator** to being installation.

2. In the **Installation Type** page, select **Custom Install** and then choose **Proxy Agents** under **Component Selection**.

3. The installer will execute the prerequisite checker; if every requirement is satisfied, the **Bypass** button will be grayed out. Click **Next** to proceed.

    ° Even if a single or a trivial requirement is not met, the installer will allow you to proceed with the installation by enabling the **Bypass** option. Do not take this route, as it is recommended to satisfy every requirement.

4. Select **Agent type** as **vSphere**.

    ° Type **Agent name** — `vRA vCenter-HUB Agent`; a Windows service will be created with this name after the installation of proxy agent.

    ° After entering the FQDN of the load balancer virtual IP for Manager Service and Web nodes, click **Test** to validate that the nodes are reachable.

    ° Enter the **Endpoint** name. You'll use this name as the endpoint name when adding the vCenter to vRA — they MUST match.

    ° Click **Add** to register the vSphere Agent type.

○ Click **Next** and then click **Install** in the next screen to begin installation:

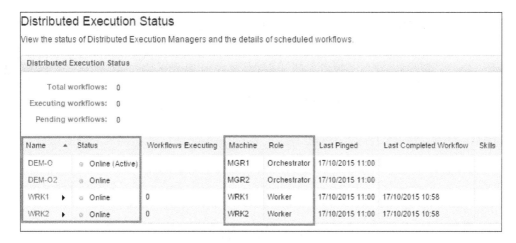

If you want to quickly validate the installation of the second DEM Orchestrator and Worker, do the following:

1. Log in to the publishing tenant portal (`https://CAFE.PKCt.LOCAL/vcac/org/Publishing`) as infrastructure administrator (`iadmin@pkct.local`).

2. Navigate to **Infrastructure | Monitoring | Distributed Execution Status**. You should see **Name** and **Status** of both DEM Orchestrator and Worker installed.

Spend some time to look at the screenshot, as it provides us some key information:

• The name and the machine FQDN of the active DEM Orchestrator node

• The names of the *online worker* nodes, the count of workflows currently being executed, and the FQDN of the machine where it is installed:

Distributed Execution Status

View the status of Distributed Execution Managers and the details of scheduled workflows.

Distributed Execution Status

Total workflows: 0
Executing workflows: 0
Pending workflows: 0

Name	Status	Workflows Executing	Machine	Role	Last Pinged	Last Completed Workflow	Skills
DEM-O	Online (Active)		MGR1	Orchestrator	17/10/2015 11:00		
DEM-O2	Online		MGR2	Orchestrator	17/10/2015 11:00		
WRK1	Online	0	WRK1	Worker	17/10/2015 11:00	17/10/2015 10:58	
WRK2	Online	0	WRK2	Worker	17/10/2015 11:00	17/10/2015 10:58	

Health monitor URL

Health monitor URLs are one of the reliable methods to check whether a service is functional. In *Chapter 2, Distributed Installation Using Custom Certificates* and this chapter, we used these URLs to verify the service status towards the end of every component configuration. I have summarized all the health monitor URLs in this section for the ease of consumption.

CAFÉ—`https://<FQDN_of_CAFE_virtual-IP_in_Loadbalancer>/vcac/ services/api/status`—in our setup, it will be `https://CAFE.PKCT.LOCAL/vcac/ services/api/status`.

> This health monitor URL will only provide the status of the `shell-ui-app` core service. If you need to find the health of all the 27 services in the CAFÉ appliance, use the following URLs:
>
> - **Via Load balancer**: `https://CAFE.PKCT.LOCAL/ component-registry/services/status/current`
> - **Via CAFÉ1 node**: `https://CAFE1.PKCT.LOCAL/ component-registry/services/status/current`
> - **Via CAFE2 node**: `https://CAFE2.PKCT.LOCAL/ component-registry/services/status/current`

- **IaaS manager data node**: `https://<FQDN_of_WEB_virtual-IP_in_ Loadbalancer>/WAPI/api/status`—in our setup—`https://WEB.PKCT. LOCAL/WAPI/api/status`

    - **Health check for WEB1 node**: `https://WEB1.PKCT.LOCAL/WAPI/ api/status`

    - **Health check for WEB2 node**: `https://WEB2.PKCT.LOCAL/WAPI/ api/status`

- **IaaS manager service node**: `https://<FQDN_of_MGR_virtual-IP_in_ Loadbalancer>/VMPS2`—in our setup—`https://MGR.PKCT.LOCAL/VMPS2`

    - Health monitor for the MGR1 node: https://MGR1.PKCT.LOCAL/ VMPS2

    - Health monitor for the MGR2 node: https://MGR2.PKCT.LOCAL/ VMPS2

- **Repository health monitor**: If you recollect from *Chapter 1, vRealize Automation and the Deconstruction of Components*, IaaS Model Manager Web is also known as repository — `https://WEB.PKCT.LOCAL/repository/data/managementmodelentities.svc`

  ° **Repository from WEB1 node**:

    `https://WEB1.PKCT.LOCAL/repository/data/managementmodelentities.svc`

  ° **Repository from WEB2 node**:

    `https://WEB2.PKCT.LOCAL/repository/data/managementmodelentities.svc`

Summary

We embarked on this chapter by testing whether the installations of the ID appliance, Postgres DB, CAFÉ appliance and the active IaaS components are, thus far, intact by creating a tenant (*Publishing*) and logging into the tenant portal (`https://CAFE.PKCT.LOCAL/vcac/org/Publishing`) as infrastructure or tenant administrator.

Once we were fully satisfied with the stability of the setup, we started configuring the remaining IaaS nodes, thereby completing the distributed installation.

In the next chapter, our focus will be towards provisioning a service catalog from the vRealize Automation self-service portal. While there are multiple steps involved before creating a service catalog, we have provided a step-by-step recipe on how to achieve it.

Since you will be introduced to many technical jargon in the next chapter, I strongly recommend that you read the vRA foundation technical guide from VMware.

`http://pubs.vmware.com/vCAC-60/topic/com.vmware.ICbase/PDF/vcloud-automation-center-60-foundations-and-concepts.pdf`.

4

Configuring a Guest OS for vRealize Automation vSphere Blueprints

Now that we have completed the installation and successfully passed the functional validation phase 1 (*Chapter 3, Functional Validation – Phase 1 and Installing Secondary Nodes*), we will continue to focus our efforts on the configuration of a **guest operating system** (**GOS**) before it can be used during the creation of a **vSphere Blueprint**.

While vRealize Automation supports several methods to provision virtual machines, we will be focusing on the following:

- **Scenario**: This provisions machines by cloning from a template object created from an existing Windows or Linux machine called the reference machine and a customization specification

- **Platform**: vSphere

- **Provisioning method**: Cloning

 For additional details on different provision methods, please read http://goo.gl/cvY5HI.

This stage is immensely important for a successful deployment of a service catalog item; otherwise, we will be spending an awful lot of time troubleshooting why a virtual machine is stuck at CustomizeOS or other stages while provisioning.

In this chapter, we will discuss the following topics:

- Guest agents: What and why?
- Learning the required steps to create a vSphere GOS template for a vRA vSphere Blueprint
- Learning about the agent installation process
  - GOS: Windows
  - GOS: Linux
- Converting a VM to a template

Guest agents

The guest agents are required to perform postprovisioning tasks inside a Windows or Linux guest operating system as a part of the vRealize Automation provisioning process. The guest agents execute after the vSphere customization specifications stage (if provided) to perform additional configuration tasks against the machine. There are three built-in features of the guest agent that are commonly used:

- Create partition, mount drives, and format additional disks added to the machine
- Configure additional network interfaces added to the machine
- Execute scripts within the guest to install applications or to perform additional configurations

 If none of the preceding features are required in your use case, installing a guest agent is not mandatory!

If the guest agent is installed in the GOS and the appropriate custom properties are configured in the blueprint, it will automatically perform the first two items as a part of the vRealize Automation provisioning process.

In order to execute scripts, you will need to tell vRealize Automation via an appropriate custom property in a blueprint or build profiles to inform the guest agents about the scripts that need to be executed.

Preparing the vSphere guest OS template

One of the significant things to be done before preparing a guest operating system as a blueprint in vRealize Automation is to ensure the supportability stance from VMware. The supportability information is detailed in `https://www.vmware.com/pdf/vrealize-automation-62-support-matrix.pdf`.

 This data will be published for every release of vRealize Automation.

In the next few pages, we will learn the *How to* of configuring a Windows guest OS and a Linux guest OS before they are attached to a blueprint.

Scope

- Windows: Windows 2012 and Windows 2008 R2
- Linux: RHEL 6.1 Server

 If a manager service component is installed in a Windows 2012 machine, ensure that you install `MS-KB-2973337` in the IaaS server. This patch is installed to gain the support for SHA512-based certificates with TLS 1.2.

The guest agent installation process is discussed in the following section:

GOS – Windows

This recipe will introduce you to the how-to steps of preparing a Windows-based guest OS for a vSphere Blueprint.

1. Log in to GOS (Windows 2012 or 2008 R2).
2. As a side note, we presume that you have installed VMware tools, time synced, and you are able to ping IaaS and the CAFÉ appliance via FQDN and IP address.
3. As a precaution, take a snapshot of this virtual machine if you would like to revert to its clean state when things go wrong.

4. Open any browser and type the FQDN/IP address of the CAFE appliance:

```
https://<IP address of CAFÉ appliance>: 5480/installer
```

 Connect to the CAFÉ node directly since the loadbalancer for CAFÉ is not configured to respond on the 5480 port.

5. Download the guest agent files under the provisioning utilities:

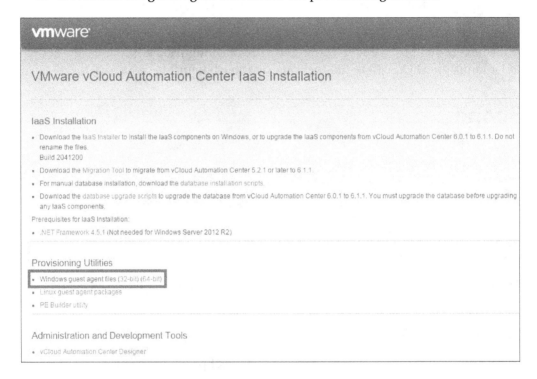

6. Right-click on the downloaded file and make sure that the contents are not blocked. If they are blocked, unblock the same:

7. Unzip the file and copy the VRMGuestagent folder to the C drive. (C:\VRMGuestAgent).

8. Open the Command Prompt by selecting **Run as administrator** to execute the following commands:

   `cd C:\VRMGuestAgent`

9. In the Command Prompt, type:

   `winservice.exe -i -h <Manager_Service server FQDN/IP>:443 -p ssl`

   ° If load balancers are not used, provide the manager service server FQDN/IP.

   ° If load balancers are used, provide the VIP and port number of the load balancer configured for the manager service server:

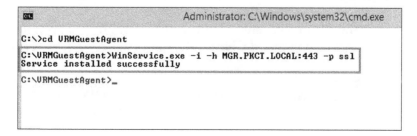

10. To verify that everything went well, check whether vCACGuestAgentService is created in Windows services and is in a **Stopped** status.

11. Start vCACGuestAgentService and navigate to the C:\VRMGuestAgent folder to validate that the cert.pem file is created with size 2 KB or 3 KB.

 If in case you see the cert.pem file in zero size, I would recommend to restart vCACGuestAgentService once more.

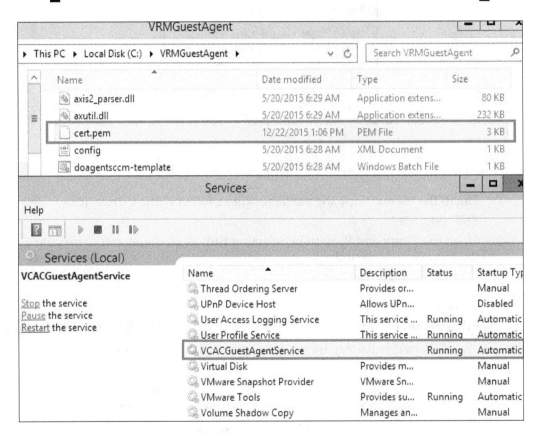

12. Power off the VM and consider taking a virtual machine snapshot if you decide to choose the **Linked Clone** option while creating a blueprint.

 This procedure also works for other supported Windows OS.

Guest agent uninstall steps

If you would like to uninstall vCACGuestAgentService as a cleanup process, follow these steps:

1. Stop vCACGuestAgentService from Windows services.

2. Uninstall the guest agent by running this elevated command:

   c:\VRMGuestAgent \WinService.exe -u

3. Restart the guest OS and then check Windows services to confirm that the guest agent is no longer present.

4. Delete the VRMGuestAgent folder to complete the cleanup process.

GOS – Linux

In this section, we will introduce you to the how-to steps of preparing a Linux based guest OS for a vSphere blueprint

1. Log in to RHEL 6.5 Server GOS (note: this procedure does work for other supported Linux OS).

> As a first step, ensure you update the OS to its latest and greatest packages. In RHEL, open a terminal windows and execute the command — yum update.
>
> As a side note, we presume that VMware Tools is installed, time synced, and we are able to ping IaaS and CAFÉ appliance via FQDN or IP address.

2. Open any browser and type the FQDN/IP address of the CAFE appliance — https://<IP address of CAFÉ appliance>: 5480/installer.

> Connect to the CAFÉ node directly since the loadbalancer for CAFÉ is not configured to respond on the 5480 port.

   ° Download the Linux guest agent packages and unzip the Linux guest agent's ZIP file to a folder on your hard drive.

   ° Identify the correct Linux guest agent file to be uploaded to the guest OS:

Since I am using a RHEL 6.1 x64 bit guest OS, I chose the x64 gugent file under the `rhel6-amd64` folder:

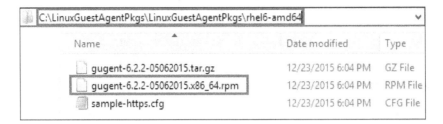

3. To make sure that the SSL certificate is available on the Linux template you are creating, open Firefox browser (or any browser of your choice) to your FQDN/IP of your *IaaS Manager Server* box and log in as administrator:

- ○ Once you have successfully provided the credentials, click the *Lock* icon in the address bar and then click **More information**
- ○ Click **View Certificate**
- ○ Click the **Details** tab
- ○ Click Export
- ○ It is important to save the certificate in the **X.509 Certificate (PEM)** format

 Please refer to the following screenshot if you have any doubts. I used Firefox browser since it's easy to export certificates.

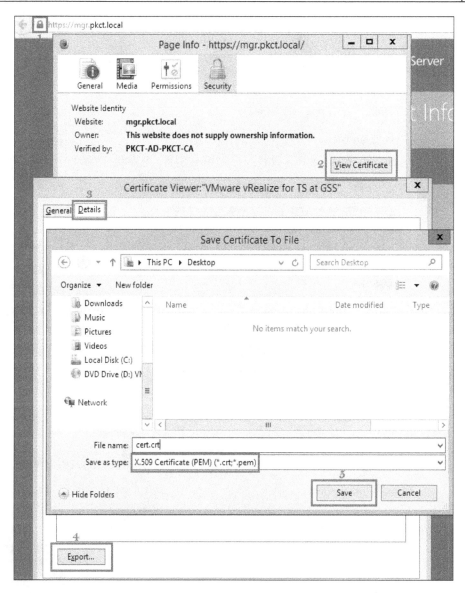

4. Install Java (`jre-1.7.0_72`) version in the `/opt/vmware-jre` folder.

   ° Download `jre-1.7.0_72-lin64.zip` from the Application Services appliance (log in as `root` and navigate to the `/home/darwin/tcserver/darwin/webapps/darwin/agent` location) *OR*.

   ° Download this file that is uploaded along with the e-version of this book.

◦ Use the WINSCP tool to transfer the `jre-1.7.0_72-lin64.zip` file to the Linux GOS in the `/tmp` folder.

Execute the following commands:

◦ Create directory:

```
mkdir -p /opt/vmware-jre
```

◦ Extract files:

```
unzip /tmp/jre-1.7.0_72-lin64.zip -d /opt/vmware-jre
```

◦ Checking JAVA version:

```
/opt/vmware-jre/bin/java -version
java version "1.7.0_72"
Java(TM) SE Runtime Environment (build 1.7.0_72-b14)
Java HotSpot(TM) 64-Bit Server VM (build 24.72-b04, mixed mode)
```

5. Use the WINSCP tool to transfer the agent file identified in step 2 and the `cert.crt` file to the Linux GOS in the `/tmp` folder.

6. Since the guest agent requires SElinux to be disabled, navigate to `/etc/sysconfig` and edit the `selinux` file and set `SELINUX` to `disabled`; quit after saving the file:

```
[root@Chap4-BP sysconfig]# cat selinux

# This file controls the state of SELinux on the system.
# SELINUX= can take one of these three values:
#       enforcing - SELinux security policy is enforced.
#       permissive - SELinux prints warnings instead of enforcing
#       disabled - No SELinux policy is loaded.
SELINUX=disabled
# SELINUXTYPE= can take one of these two values:
#       targeted - Targeted processes are protected,
#       mls - Multi Level Security protection.
SELINUXTYPE=targeted


[root@Chap4-BP sysconfig]#
```

7. Installing the guest agent:

◦ I have executed a series of commands and captured the screenshot for easy understanding.

° SSH to the Linux guest OS and navigate to the `/tmp` directory:

```
[root@Chap4-BP tmp]# rpm -i gugent-6.2.2-05062015.x86_64.rpm
[root@Chap4-BP tmp]# cp cert.crt /usr/share/gugent/
[root@Chap4-BP tmp]# cd /usr/share/gugent/
[root@Chap4-BP gugent]# openssl x509 -in cert.crt -out cert.pem -outform PEM
[root@Chap4-BP gugent]# ls
axis2      cert.pem      gugent.properties
cert.crt   config.xml                    site
[root@Chap4-BP gugent]# ./installgugent.sh MGR.PKCT.LOCAL:443 ssl
chkconfig
[root@Chap4-BP gugent]#
```

8. To check whether the configuration is correct, execute the `rungugent.sh` script and verify that the endpoint is pointing to `https://FQDN/IP-of-Iaas-Manager-Service-Node/VMPS2` (`https://MGR.PKCT.LOCAL/VMPS2`) and your output matches the screenshot except for the endpoint names:

```
[root@Chap4-BP gugent]# ./rungugent.sh
Application.MachineQuery: [Information] uuid = 421ec03a-3997-6590-0352-6366225aeb15
Application: [Debug] Using the network enabled proxy ...
Application: [Debug] The vCAC endpoint is https://mgr.pkct.local:443/VMPS2
Application: [Debug] The AXIS2C directory is axis2/.
Application: [Debug] Requesting work for agent ID 3ac01e42-9739-9065-0352-6366225aeb15.
Application: [Debug] Fetching a work item ...
Application.Proxy: [Debug]




Application.Proxy: [Debug] No workitem currently available




Application: [Debug] Requesting work for agent ID 421ec03a-3997-6590-0352-6366225aeb15.
Application: [Debug] Fetching a work item ...
Application.Proxy: [Debug]




Application.Proxy: [Debug] No workitem currently available




Application: [Debug] Uninitializing subsystem: Logging Subsystem
^C
[root@Chap4-BP gugent]#
```

9. If you are using RHEL/CentOS as a guest OS for cloning, execute the following commands as the last steps before shutting down the VM:

```
touch /.unconfigured
rm -f /etc/ssh/ssh_host_*
ifdown eth0
sed -i '/^HWADDR=.*$/d' /etc/sysconfig/network-scripts/ifcfg-eth0
ifup eth0
rm -f /etc/udev/rules.d/70-persistent-net.rules
shutdown -h no
```

Converting the VM to a template

Once you have completed the preceding steps, decide whether you would like to convert the virtual machine to a template or not. Please read http://goo.gl/YaBlR3 to identify which of the previous options you would choose in your environment.

- If the **Clone** option is selected in **Action** while configuring the vSphere Blueprint, a virtual machine template is required as input
- If the **Linked Clone** option is selected in **Action** while configuring the vSphere blueprint, a virtual machine with a snapshot is required as input

Summary

Well, that brings us to a successful completion of configuring a guest operating system before it could be used for a vRealize Automation vSphere Blueprint!

While a blueprint varies based on the platform type, this chapter is focused on learning how to configure a vSphere template. We decided to spend some quality time here; otherwise, the deployment of a service catalog can be impacted if the configuration is flawed.

To recap, we have successfully installed all the nodes in the vRealize automation distributed architecture followed by a functional validation (phase 1). Now that we have learned how to configure a vSphere template for blueprint use, we will proceed to the next chapter and provision a service catalog and finish the second phase of validation.

5
Functional Validation – Phase 2 and Zero to VM Provisioning

Every installation needs to be functionally validated before approving the acceptance of the configuration. To summarize, the earlier chapters assisted us in successfully installing the vRealize automation distributed setup. Nevertheless, we are not done until we functionally corroborate whether the setup is operational. This chapter will talk about how to prepare the environment and then execute the functional test.

We will look at how to create a service catalog item before the user deploys it via the vRA self-service portal. If the deployment is successful, we can be assured that we are headed in the right direction. I also wanted to highlight the list of topics that will be discussed in this chapter:

- Providing the required permissions in the vSphere Endpoint
- Creating and configuring credentials
- Configuring a vSphere Endpoint
- Login validation
- Configuring fabric groups
- Configuring a machine prefix
- Creating business groups
- Configuring reservation policies
- Configuring a VM template and VM customization spec in vCenter
- Creating a vSphere blueprint

- Creating a service
- Configuring a catalog item
- Creating an entitlement
- Requesting a service catalog
- Monitoring deployment status

An overview of creating a service catalog

Since creating a service catalog involves multiple steps, we have designed a schematic in a logical sequence for easy understanding. Please take some time to review it:

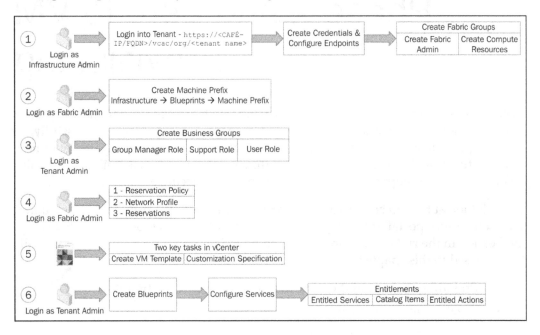

Providing the required permissions in the vSphere Endpoint

Before adding an endpoint, make sure you have granted the administrator role access at the root level in the vCenter Server for the service account that will used in the vRA credentials page. In my case, I will be using **PKCT \ Administrator**:

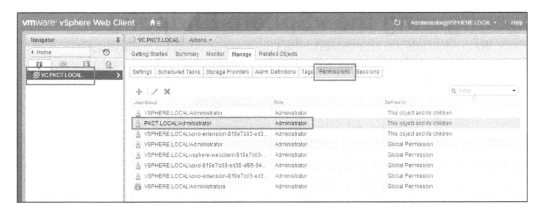

 On completing the installation of all the vRA components, restart all the active and passive nodes before you begin the configuration followed by the functional validation.

Creating and configuring credentials

Log in to the vRA portal (`https://CAFE-LB-IP-or-FQDN/vcac/org/tenantname`) as an **Infrastructure administrator** and navigate to the **Credentials** page; to add credentials, click **New Credentials**. If you are planning to add multiple endpoints, ensure that you add some text to the description field for clarity:

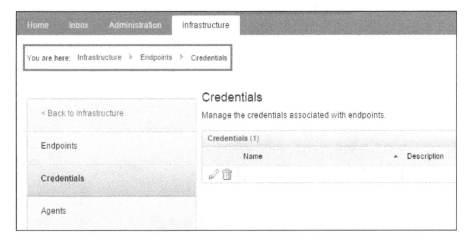

Configuring the vSphere Endpoint

Once the credentials are created, add the vSphere endpoint by navigating to **Endpoints** in the **Infrastructure** tab. Click **New Endpoint** and browse to **Virtual | vSphere (vCenter)**:

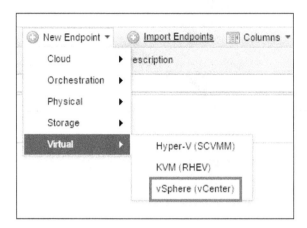

Enter the details as shown in the following screenshot:

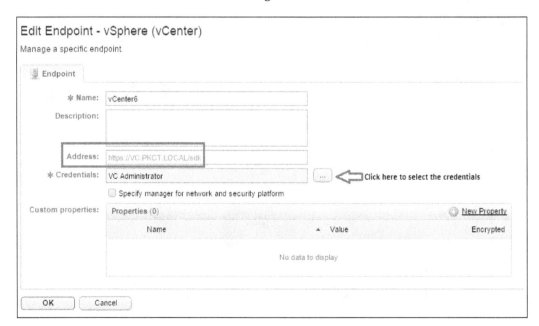

While adding vCenter as an Endpoint, it's worth noting a few items:

1. Add /sdk (lowercase) towards the end of IP/FQDN of vCenter.

2. You *should* use the same name that was used at the time of installing the vSphere proxy agent. If you fail to recollect the name, you may navigate to **Infrastructure | Monitoring | Log**; you will find an error similar to the following screenshot. Anything within the vRA and agent texts will be the agent name:

Login validation

You should not see any errors for **VRM Agent** when you navigate to **Infrastructure | Monitoring | Log** after the endpoint configuration (refer to the following screenshot):

Error	11/09/2015 14:26	VRM Agent	vRA vCenter6 Agent-IAAS-WRKR2	PKCT\administrator	IAAS-WRKR2	This exception was caught: Cannot complete login due to an incorrect user name or password.
Error	10/09/2015 13:55	VRM Agent	vRA vCenter6 Agent-IAAS-WRKR2	PKCT\administrator	IAAS-WRKR2	This exception was caught: Cannot complete login due to an incorrect user name or password.

Proxy agents will fail the data collection process if the **VRM Agent** login fails.

 Data collection may fail if the user does not have enough permission on the configured endpoint – do not skip the steps under the *Providing the required permissions in the vSphere Endpoint* topic in this chapter.

Configuring fabric groups

While you are still logged in as an **Infrastructure administrator**, do the following:

1. Navigate to **Infrastructure | Groups | Fabric Groups**.
2. Click on the **New Fabric Group** option.

3. Add a fabric administrator, select the **Compute resources** for VM provisioning, and click **OK** to conclude this step:

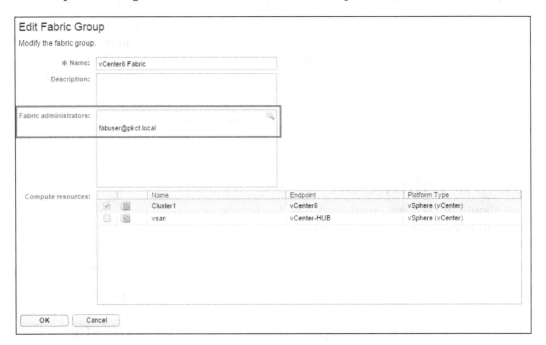

 An empty list under the **Compute resources** inventory means that the data collection process by the proxy agent failed due to either invalid credentials or insufficient permission. Please look at **Infrastructure | Monitoring | Log** for the failure information.

Configuring the machine prefix

Here are the steps to configure a machine prefix:

1. Log out as the **Infrastructure administrator** from the vRA portal (https://CAFE-IP-or-FQDN/vcac/org/tenantname).

2. Log in to the vRA portal as **Fabric User**.

3. Navigate to **Infrastructure | Blueprints | Machine Prefixes**.

4. Click **New Machine Prefix** and fill in the relevant details:

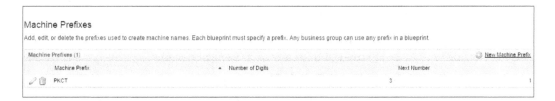

Creating business groups

Here are the steps to create business groups:

1. Log out as **Fabric User** from the vRA portal (`https://CAFE-IP-or-FQDN/vcac/org/tenantname`).

2. Log in to the vRA portal as **Tenant Administrator**.

3. Navigate to **Infrastructure | Groups | Business Groups**.

4. Click **New Business Group** and fill in the relevant details.

5. Click **OK** to conclude this step:

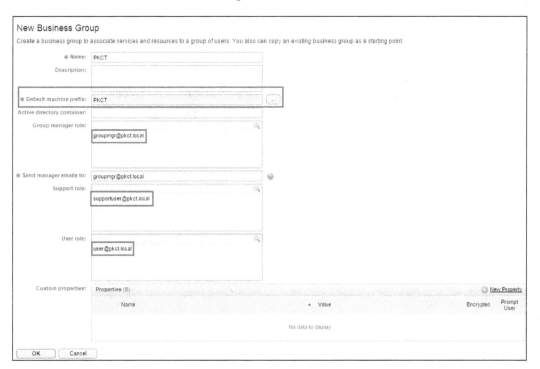

Configuring reservation policies

Here are the steps to configure reservation policies:

1. Log out as **Infrastructure administrator** from the vRA portal (https://CAFE-IP-or-FQDN/vcac/org/tenantname).

2. Log in to the vRA portal as **Fabric User**.

3. Navigate to **Infrastructure | Reservations | Reservation Policies**.

4. Click **New Reservation Policy**, fill in the details, and click the green check icon to save the details.

5. Click **New Storage Reservation Policy**, fill in the details, and click the green check icon to save the details:

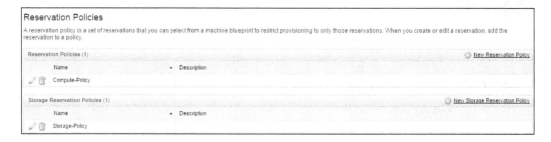

6. Configuring network profiles:

    1. Continue this step while logged in as **Fabric User**.

    2. Navigate to **Infrastructure | Reservations | Network Profiles**.

    3. Click **New Network Profile** and select **External**.

4. Fill in the required details for both, the **Network Profile Information** tab and the **IP Ranges** tab.

5. Click **OK** to conclude this step:

Edit Network Profile - External

Edit a network profile for managing ranges of static IPv4 network addresses.

| Network Profile Information | IP Ranges |

* Name: `LAN`

Description:

* Subnet mask: `255.255.252.0`

Gateway:

DNS / WINS

Primary DNS:

Secondary DNS:

DNS suffix:

DNS search suffix:

Preferred WINS:

Alternate WINS:

6. Click the **IP Ranges** tab to add the static IP range to be used by the service catalogs during deployment.

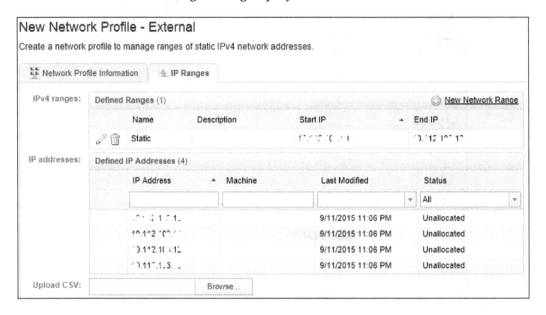

7. Configure reservations:

    1. Continue this step while you are still logged in as **Fabric User**.

    2. Navigate to **Infrastructure | Reservations | Reservations**.

    3. Go to **New Reservation | Virtual | vSphere (vCenter)**.

    4. Fill in the details for the **Reservation Information**, **Resources**, and **Network** tabs.

    5. Click **OK** once you have finished step 1, 2, and 3:

6. Click the **Resources** tab to configure or allocate the memory and storage resources:

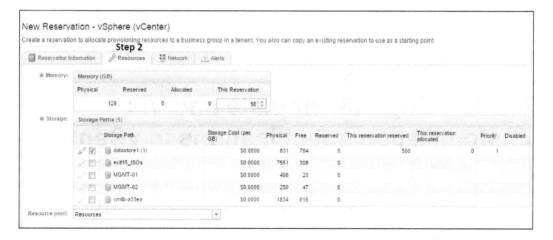

If you don't see any memory or storage details, it could mean that the data collection has not yet been completed. Either wait for some time (*data collection takes more time if the inventory size is huge*) or log in as **Infrastructure administrator** and navigate to **Infrastructure | Monitoring | Log** and check for any errors related to **Manager Service** under **Instance Name**. I faced this challenge in my setup and found the following log excerpt:

DataBaseStatsService: ignoring exception: Error executing query usp_SelectAgent Inner Exception: Error executing query usp_SelectAgentCapabilities

Since the log page provides the node information from where the error is initiated, it was easy for me to dig into the logs to identify the offending module—the MSTDC module. Restarting the *distributed transaction coordinator* solved this issue. This is one of the reasons why we recommended that you restart all the nodes after installation.

Configuring VM template and VM customization specifications in vCenter

Here are the steps to configure a VM template and VM customization specifications in vCenter:

1. Log in to the vCenter Server as administrator and create a VM for blueprint use (refer to *Chapter 4, Configuring a Guest OS for vRealize Automation vSphere Blueprints* for more details).

2. Create a VM snapshot in the vCenter server if **Linked Clone** will be used while creating a vRA Blueprint.

3. Using the customization specifications manager in vCenter creates a customization spec.

Creating a vSphere blueprint

Here are the steps to create a vSphere blueprint:

1. Log out as **Fabric User** from the vRA portal (`https://CAFE-IP-or-FQDN/vcac/org/tenantname`).

2. Log in to vRA portal as **Tenant Administrator** or as a **Business Group** user:

 Blueprint will be accessible by every **Business Group** in a **Tenant** if it is created using a **Tenant** admin. Likewise, if you wish to allow blueprint access to users within a **Business Group**, log in as a business group user and create a blueprint.

3. Let's navigate to **Infrastructure | Blueprints | Blueprints**.

4. Select **New Blueprint | Virtual | vSphere (vCenter)**:

5. The first step in creating a blueprint is to start with **Blueprint Information**:

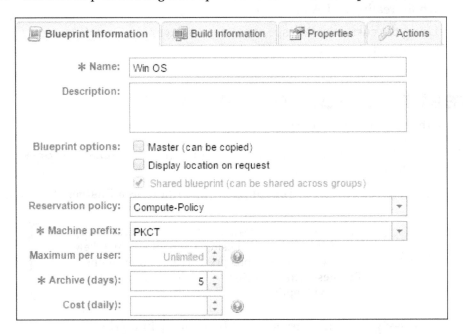

6. Click on the **Build Information** tab:

   1. Select the **Linked Clone** option for faster provision and other storage benefits.

   2. The name used in vCenter customization specification manager and customization spec should match.

   3. Keep the settings in the **Properties** and **Actions** tabs to defaults unless you want to change them.

   4. Click **OK** to conclude this step, as we are not using any additional properties or actions:

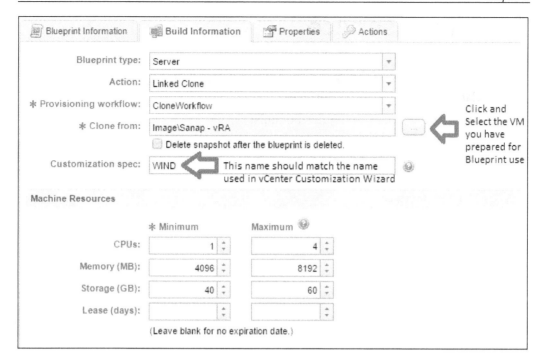

7. Publish the blueprint as follows:

   1. Navigate to **Infrastructure | Blueprints | Blueprints**.
   2. Select the create blueprint and click **Publish**.
   3. Create **OK** to conclude this step.

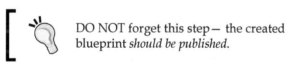

DO NOT forget this step— the created blueprint *should be published*.

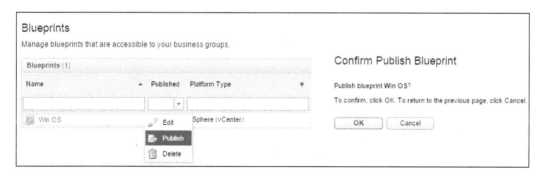

Creating a service

Here are the steps to create a service:

1. While logged in as a **Tenant administrator**, navigate to **Administration | Catalog Management | Services**.

2. Click **Add** and fill the required details:

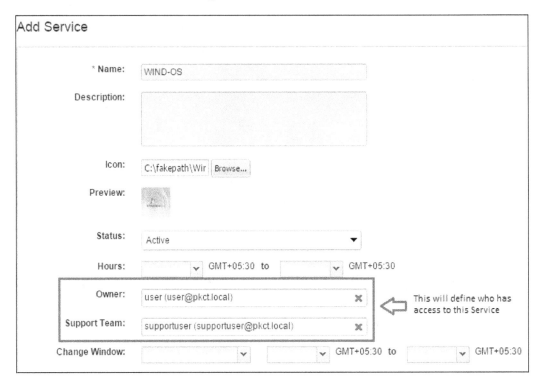

You can check the status of the service as shown in the following screenshot:

Configuring a catalog item

In this section, we will be mapping the vSphere blueprint, which was created in the previous step, to a service:

1. If you are still logged in as a **Tenant administrator**, navigate to **Administration | Catalog Management | Catalog Items**.

2. You should see the blueprint (**Win OS**) listed here.

3. Click **Win OS** and map it to the service (WIND OS) created in the earlier step:

   Before:

   After:

Creating an entitlement

This is the last step before provisioning a service catalog item:

1. While logged in as a **Tenant administrator**, navigate to **Administration | Catalog Management | Entitlements**.

2. Click **Add** and fill the required details and click **Next**:

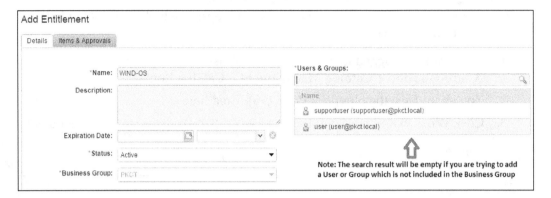

3. Click **Entitled Services** and select the **WIND-OS** service:

4. Click **Entitled Catalog Item** and select the **Win-OS** blueprint:

5. Click **Entitled Actions** and select the actions according to your requirements and choice:

6. Click **Add** to conclude this step; your final screen should look similar to the following screenshot:

Just to recap, we started this chapter in an effort to confirm whether our installation will enable the users to deploy a service catalog item via the self-service portal of vRA. Until now, we have spent time in creating a service catalog item. In the next few pages, let's check how to monitor deployment progress once a user requests for a service catalog.

Requesting a service catalog

We are at the final stage where we will perform functional validation by requesting a service catalog item from the vRealize Automation self-service portal:

1. Log out as **Tenant administrator** from the vRA portal (`https://CAFE-IP-or-FQDN/vcac/org/tenantname`).

2. Log in as a user (or whoever has the permission to deploy the catalog item) in the vRA self-service portal.

3. Navigate to the **Catalog** tab:

4. Click **Request**. A review page of the VM configuration will be displayed.

5. Click **Submit** if you are satisfied with the configuration, or make changes and click **Submit**.

Monitoring deployment status

The deployment status of the service catalog can be monitored either by the user from the self-service portal or by the fabric administrator.

Monitoring deployment by a user

The only way a user can monitor the progress of deployment is via the **Request** tab in the CAFÉ self-service portal.

A successful deployment results in the status changing to **Successful**.

In-progress status:

Successful status:

Monitoring deployment by fabric administrator

The administrator can monitor the deployment by logging to vRA CAFÉ portal as fabric user.

1. Navigate to **Infrastructure | Machines | Managed Machines**.

2. The virtual machine deployment has to go through various statuses; I have captured some of them for your reference:

    ° Requested - Starting

    ° CloneMachine

    ° CustomizeMachine

    ° Initial PowerOn

    ° CustomizeOS

    ° MachineProvisioned

    ° TurningOn

    ° On - Final

3. The **On** status is the result of a successful deployment:

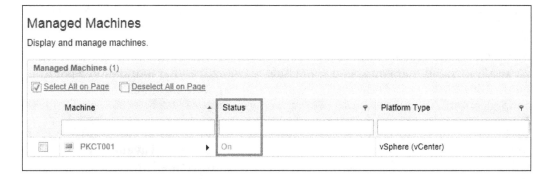

Things to remember

Every installation needs to be functionally validated before approving the acceptance of a configuration.

While configuring an endpoint, business group, fabric group, and blueprint, you may encounter a few challenges. I wanted to touch upon some of my experiences of such challenges:

- On completing the installation of all the vRA components, restart all the active nodes before you begin the functional validation.

- While configuring an endpoint, ensure the user has privileges at the root folder in vCenter.

- Since the errors are not thrown upfront while configuring an endpoint, check (**Infrastructure | Monitoring | Log**) for any endpoint-related errors and fix them.

- It is recommended to add user groups while configuring business groups for the ease of administration.

- Log in as **Infrastructure administrator** to the vRA portal (`https://cafe.pkct.local/vcac/org/Publishing`) in a dedicated browser until you finish the validation; otherwise, you need to frequently log (out/in) if a single browser is used for all the users until the end of all the configurations.

- The names used in the vCenter customization specification manager and customization spec while configuring the blueprint should match.

Summary

To summarize, we have spent time learning the step-by-step recipe on how to create a service catalog item in this chapter. To calibrate the deployment, the service catalog should be deployed successfully. If it is, we can confirm that the deployment and configuration are headed in the correct direction.

By the end of *Chapter 3, Functional Validation – Phase 1 and Installing Secondary Nodes* we recommended that you spend some time learning the vRA foundation technical guide from VMware to understand the technical jargon used in this chapter — `http://pubs.vmware.com/vCAC-60/topic/com.vmware.ICbase/PDF/vcloud-automation-center-60-foundations-and-concepts.pdf`.

In the next chapter, you will spend some time learning the high availability and failover process for each component in the vRealize distributed architecture. Testing the failover for every component is mandatory, and the recipe for a successful failover is to follow the steps in a logical sequence.

6
Testing Failover Scenarios for vRealize Automation Components

Firstly, I want you relax as we have completed the most composite portion of the installation. However, the job is not yet done. As you can imagine, a failover can have multiple meanings in the world of IT. I would like to elucidate this before we go forward; here, failover refers to the process of promoting the passive node to an active node in a event where the active node fails.

Having meticulously designed the high availability for all the components in vRealize Automation, it's imperative that we comprehend the technicalities around it:

- Understanding the HA mode for all components in vRealize Automation
- Identifying active nodes in the current state
- How to identify whether the active component failed
- How to promote a passive component in the event the active component fails

The following topics will be covered in this chapter:

- Failover of vPostgres
- Failover of vRA CAFÉ appliances
- Failover of Model Manager Web
- Failover of Manager Service
- Failover of DEM Orchestrator
- Failover of DEM Worker
- Failover of proxy agents

vRealize Automation components and HA modes

vRealize Automation components in a high availability cluster are groups of computers that support server applications that can be reliably utilized with a minimum downtime. They operate in HA mode to harness redundant computers in groups that provide a continued service when system components fail. Without high availability, if a server running a particular application crashes, the application will be unavailable until the crashed server is fixed:

vRealize Components	HA Modes	Failover Type
CAFE	Active – Active	Automatic
Postgres Database	Active – Passive	Manual
IaaS Manager Service	Active – Passive	Manual
IaaS Web Server	Active – Active	Automatic
DEM Orchestrator	Active – Passive	Automatic
DEM Worker	Active – Active	Automatic
Proxy Agents	Active – Active	Automatic

Active-Active configuration

All nodes are in active mode while handling the alike function on the same state. If there is a failure of one active node, then the other active node automatically handles the traffic. After the restoration of the failed node, it will enter the active mode routinely, where the load will be shared between the nodes. However, this depends on the session persistence settings used in the load balancer. CAFÉ, IaaS web server, DEM Worker, and proxy agents comes under this category. Since the failover types for the aforementioned components are automatic, the failover process is effortless. Nevertheless, if all the active nodes go down, a specific sequence of steps should be followed before the first node is brought online. We will talk about this in detail later in the chapter.

Active-Passive configuration

Only one node is in active mode, while the others will be in passive. When an issue is identified on the active system, the passive node will take the place of the active node; the failover process can be either manual or automatic:

- Postgres and IaaS Manager Server come under this category with the failover type set to manual.

- DEM Orchestrator also falls into this category with the failover type programmed to be automatic. The standby DEM Orchestrator is designed to poll the health of the active DEM Orchestrator via the IaaS database to promote itself to an active role. It will continue to be in the active role even if the failed node comes online (no failback).

- Promoting a passive node to an active role demands a logical sequence to be carried out for a successful failover, which will be discussed later in this chapter.

Failover of the identity management appliance

The identity management appliance does not provide any high availability features out of the box. However, we should be considering one or all of the following options:

- Leverage vSphere HA as the first option.

- The IDM appliance can be FT (vSphere) protected along with vSphere HA. The good news about vSphere 6.0 is that FT supports up to 4 vCPUs.

More details on vSphere FT can be found at `http://kb.vmware.com/kb/1013428`

Failover of vPostgres

By now, we have understood that Postgres database follows the active-passive HA configuration with the manual failover process. This means that if the active node fails, the passive node can only be brought back online by manual steps. Postgres provides us with two choices (NSX load balancer and web-based) to identify which node is acting as a master or slave.

Choice 1 – identify active node via NSX load balancer

The first option is to do this via the NSX load balancer:

1. Log in to vCenter Web Client and navigate to the **Networking & Security** tab.

2. Click on **NSX Edges** and select the edge node where the load balancer service is enabled.

3. Click the **Pools** option and click **Show Pool Statistics** (in this screenshot, both the CAFÉ nodes are active).

4. Select the **Postgres_Pool** configuration, which lists the nodes and their statuses:

 If you recollect from *Chapter 2, Distributed Installation Using Custom Certificates* we added a passive (PG2) node and unchecked the **Enable Member** option in the pools configuration page since the passive database node cannot accept any SQL transactions.

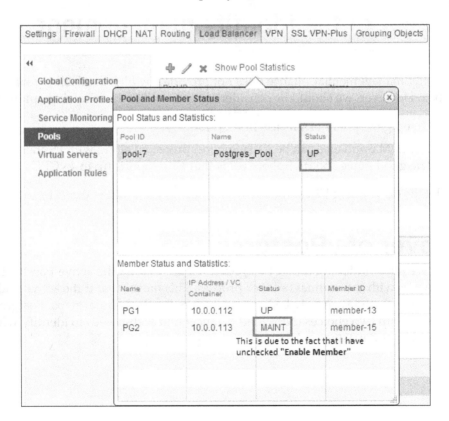

Choice 2 – identify master node via health monitor URL

The other option is to browse the FQDN of the Postgres database nodes directly (*not via the load balancer virtual IP*). Since both the nodes have been configured with the monitor scripts, depending who is the master, you will receive a response as shown in the screenshot:

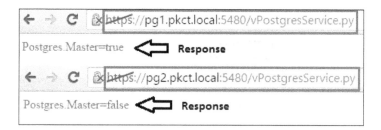

Along with to this, VMware has published an excellent KB (kb.vmware.com/ kb/2108923) article about how to promote a slave to master and vice versa. Since this documentation is precise and useful, we will skip this topic.

Failover of CAFÉ appliance

The HA design for the CAFÉ appliance is active-active; since the failover mode is automatic, if one node goes down, the other node will persist to service the client requests without any special configuration.

I would like to succinctly talk about two states followed by the logical sequence of the steps necessary to recover if the active node goes down:

- **State 1**: Failure of one active node
- **State 2**: Failure of all the active nodes

The CAFÉ health monitor URL

The current state of the CAFÉ nodes can be gathered using the health monitor URL. Open the browser and navigate to `https://<CAFE-Loadbalance-IP-or-FQDN>/vcac/services/api/status`, that is `https://CAFE.PKCT.LOCAL/vcac/services/api/status`. If both or one of the nodes are active, you should receive a response as shown in the following screenshot:

```
▼<serviceRegistryStatus>
  ▼<identityCertificateInfo>
     <identityCertificateExists>true</identityCertificateExists>
     <issuerName>CN=cafe-b26fb237-ef8a-4627-a7da-c0ee438f46c3</issuerName>
     <notValidAfter>2017-10-05T20:50:24+05:30</notValidAfter>
     <notValidBefore>2015-10-06T20:50:24+05:30</notValidBefore>
     <principalName>CN=cafe-b26fb237-ef8a-4627-a7da-c0ee438f46c3</principalName>
  ▼<thumbprint>
        80:F2:4E:66:23:BE:9E:1B:40:4E:16:DC:B5:A1:48:7B:10:E2:52:A2
     </thumbprint>
  </identityCertificateInfo>
  <initialized>true</initialized>
  <serviceInitializationStatus>REGISTERED</serviceInitializationStatus>
  <serviceName>shell-ui-app</serviceName>
  <solutionUser>cafe-b26fb237-ef8a-4627-a7da-c0ee438f46c3</solutionUser>
  <startedTime>2015-10-17T19:10:33.904+05:30</startedTime>
  <serviceRegistrationId>ff333550-041e-47da-8671-7fb57fd93e0c</serviceRegistrationId>
  ▼<sslCertificateInfo>
     <identityCertificateExists>true</identityCertificateExists>
     <issuerName>CN=PKCT-AD-PKCT-CA,DC=PKCT,DC=LOCAL</issuerName>
     <notValidAfter>2017-10-07T19:59:25+05:30</notValidAfter>
     <notValidBefore>2015-10-07T19:49:25+05:30</notValidBefore>
  ▼<principalName>
        CN=VMware vRealize for TS at GSS,OU=TS,O=GSS,L=BNG,ST=KA,C=IN
     </principalName>
  ▼<thumbprint>
        4A:18:6D:34:29:82:2F:22:01:A6:58:48:60:F0:ED:DB:6B:07:11:56
     </thumbprint>
  </sslCertificateInfo>
</serviceRegistryStatus>
```

Which CAFÉ node is active?

The only UI option to find the active CAFÉ nodes is through the NSX Edge load balancer pools page:

1. Log in to vCenter Web Client and navigate to the **Networking & Security** tab.

2. Click on **NSX Edges** and select the edge node where the load balancer service is enabled.

3. Click the **Pools** option and click **Show Pool Statistics** (in this screenshot, both the CAFÉ nodes are active):

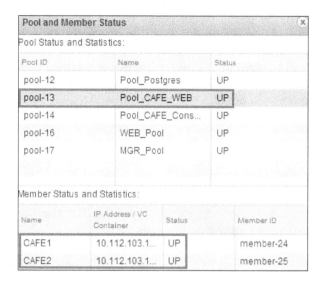

However, the current limitation is that we don't have an UI option to find which CAFÉ appliance is currently servicing the clients.

Failover test – state 1 (one active node failed)

To simulate the failure, we will either power off or disconnect vNIC of one CAFÉ node:

- Wait for some time and check whether you are able to access the health monitor URL (`https://CAFE.PKCT.LOCAL/vcac/services/api/status`) – you should receive a response as shown in the screenshot in the topic, The CAFÉ health monitor URL of this chapter once all the services have started

- The **Pools** page of the NSX Edge load balancer should show one node in **DOWN** status

Since there are no special steps required for the failover, this seems a fairly simple process.

Failover test – state 2 (failure of all the active nodes)

In a situation where every active node failed due to a datacenter-wide power outage or shutdown due to maintenance operation, bringing the first active node online is not a simple process. We need to follow a sequence of steps to bring the first node online. Once the first node is up, bringing the successive nodes should be quicker. Let's look at the sequence in detail.

It is assumed that dependent services such as the Postgres database and identity management machines are already powered on and fully functional:

1. Before powering on the first CAFÉ node, update the CAFÉ NSX load balancer **Service Monitoring** setting:

   ○ **Service Monitoring configuration**: Update the existing configuration to reflect the following changes:

Name	Interval	Timeout	Retries	Type	Method	URL	Receive
CAFÉ_SM	5	10	3	TCP			

2. Once the first CAFÉ node is up and all the services have started, open the browser and go to the health monitor URL: `https://CAFE.PKCT.LOCAL/vcac/services/api/status`. If you receive a **REGISTERED** response for the `shell-ui-app` service, proceed to the next step else wait until this is achieved.

3. Update the CAFÉ NSX load balancer **Service Monitoring** setting to the following:

   ○ **Service Monitoring configuration**: Update the existing configuration to reflect the following changes:

Name	Interval	Timeout	Retries	Type	Method	URL	Receive:
CAFÉ_SM	5	10	3	HTTPS	GET	/vcac/services/api/status	REGISTERED

4. Proceed to power on the remaining CAFÉ nodes.

You could also connect to the health monitor page of the CAFÉ nodes directly to check the status of all the services:

CAFE1 node: `https://CAFE1.PKCT.LOCAL/component-registry/services/status/current?limit=256`

CAFE2 node: `https://CAFE2.PKCT.LOCAL/component-registry/services/status/current?limit=256`

This concludes the failover testing for the CAFÉ nodes.

Failover of Model Manager Web

The Web nodes fall under the active-active HA design with the failover taking place automatically if the active node fails. If the Web node, where the Model Manager Data is installed goes down, the impact will be visible during the following:

- vRealize Automation upgrade
- Executing the register solution `rser` and `RepoUtil` commands

When any or one Model Manager Web node goes down, the failover process is straightforward and seamless. Unlike CAFÉ or Manager Service, there are no special instructions required to recover the nodes if all the Web nodes fail due to any datacenter-wide crash or maintenance activities.

At any time, use the health monitor URL to check the status of the node:

- **IaaS Manager Node**: `https://<FQDN_of_WEB_virtual-IP_in_Loadbalancer>/WAPI/api/status` — in our setup it will be — `https://WEB.PKCT.LOCAL/WAPI/api/status`

If at least one node is active behind the load balancer, you should receive a response similar to the following screenshot:

```
This XML file does not appear to have any style information associated with it. The document tree is shown below.

▼<ServiceRegistryStatus xmlns:i="http://www.w3.org/2001/XMLSchema-instance" xmlns="http://schemas.datacontract.org/2004/07/DynamicOps.Api.Model">
   <DefaultServiceEndpointType>com.vmware.csp.iaas.api</DefaultServiceEndpointType>
   <ErrorMessage i:nil="true"/>
   <IdentityCertificateInfo i:nil="true"/>
   <Initialized>true</Initialized>
   <ServiceInitializationStatus>REGISTERED</ServiceInitializationStatus>
   <ServiceName>iaas-service</ServiceName>
   <ServiceRegistrationId i:nil="true"/>
   <SolutionUser i:nil="true"/>
   <SslCertificateInfo i:nil="true"/>
   <StartedTime i:nil="true"/>
</ServiceRegistryStatus>
```

To access the nodes directly, use the following health monitor URLs:

- **Health check for the WEB1 node**: `https://WEB1.PKCT.LOCAL/WAPI/api/ status`

- **Health check for the WEB2 node**: `https://WEB2.PKCT.LOCAL/WAPI/api/ status`

Failover of Manager Service

Since the Manager Service falls under the active-passive HA design, at any point in time, only one node can play an active role.

Finding the active node

It is easy to identify which Manager Service node is currently active using the following options:

- **Browse the URL**: `https://<FQDN-of-of-loadbalancer-virtual-IP>/ VMPS2`, that is, `https://MGR.PKCT.LOCAL/VPMS2`. Go to the end of the XML output and look for the **soap:address location** keyword, which reveals the FQDN of the machine where the Manager Service is active:

```
- <wsdl:service name="GuestAgentWorkItemService">
    - <wsdl:port name="BasicHttpBinding_VMPSProxyAgent" binding="tns:BasicHttpBinding_VMPSProxyAgent">
        <soap:address location="https://mgr1.pkct.local/VPMS2"/>
      </wsdl:port>
  </wsdl:service>
</wsdl:definitions>
```

- Via the NSX load balancer, do the following:
    1. Log in to vCenter Web Client and navigate to the **Networking & Security** tab
    2. Click on **NSX Edges** and select the edge node where the load balancer service is enabled

3. Click the **Pools** option and click **Show Pool Statistics** (in this screenshot, both the CAFÉ nodes are active):

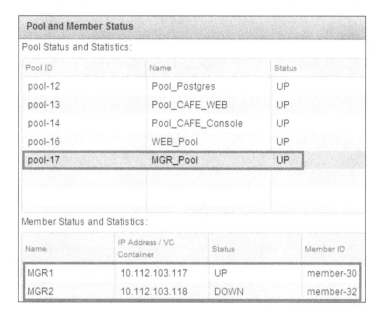

Failover test

To simulate the failure, we stopped the service (*VMware vCloud Automation Center Service*) from `service.msc` MMC in the active (`MGR1`) node.

Symptoms

Here is the list of operations that will fail if the active nodes or the Manager Service (VMware vCloud Automation Center Service) is stopped:

- Lifecycle operations (provision, power on and off, reconfigure, and destroy)
- Virtual machine observer
- Inventory/state/performance data will fail to trigger
- Data collection process for any hypervisor using proxy agents

Effect and failover step

Using the health monitor URL, check whether the service is down—`https://<FQDN-of-of-loadbalancer-virtual-IP>/VMPS2`; our setup will be using—`https://MGR.PKCT.LOCAL/VMPS2`:

- If the web browser loads the **Page can't be displayed** page, there can be two probabilities:
    - ○ Either the service is down
    - ○ The load balancer is failing to route to the active Manager Service node

- To additionally support the service down situation, you should receive **404 - File or directory not found**. in the web browser after providing the credentials by accessing the health monitor URL of the active node directly—`https://MGR1.PKCT.LOCAL/VMPS2`.

Let's take a look at the steps involved in the failover process once the preceding conditions are met:

1. If the primary server is still running, set the vCloud Automation Center Service to manual startup.

2. Deactivate the active server (which is currently in down state) in the NSX load balancer (uncheck the **Enable Member** for the Manager Service node that shows **DOWN** state in the **Pools** page):

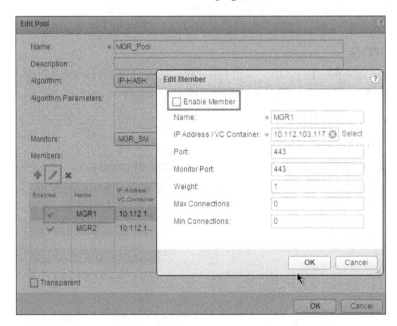

3. Connect to the passive node via RDP and open Command Prompt with administrator access and type `iisreset`.

4. Open **Services** and start the vCloud Automation Center Services.

5. Set the **vCloud Automation Center Service** startup type to **Automatic**.

6. Restart all the agent services and DEM worker services on all the other servers in the architecture.

> If the failed active node comes online, set the **vCloud Automation Center** service to manual startup if not done and leave the setup as it is. The passive node that was promoted to an active role will continue to function as an active node until it fails. In short, there is no failback even if the original active node comes online.

Failover of DEM Orchestrator

DEM Orchestrator works in the active-passive configuration and the passive DEM Orchestrator service is promoted to an active role automatically if the active DEM Orchestrator service fails.

The standby DEM Orchestrator is designed to poll the health of an active DEM Orchestrator via the IaaS database; once the status of the active DEM Orchestrator is marked offline in the database, the standby DEM will be instantly promoted to take over the active role. It will continue to be in the active role even if the failed node comes online (no failback).

Which DEM Orchestrator is online and active?

It is quite easy to identify which DEM Orchestrator node is active and online; here are the steps:

1. Log in to the tenant portal (`https://CAFE.PKCt.LOCAL/vcac/org/Publishing`) as an Infrastructure administrator (`iadmin@pkct.local`).

2. Navigate to **Infrastructure | Monitoring | Distributed Execution Status**. **Name** and **Status** of all the DEM Orchestrators and Workers will be listed.

Let's review some interesting details from the screenshot:

- The DEM Orchestrator service name used at the time of installation will be listed under the **Name** column

- The **Machine** column populates the machine name where the DEM Orchestrator service is installed:

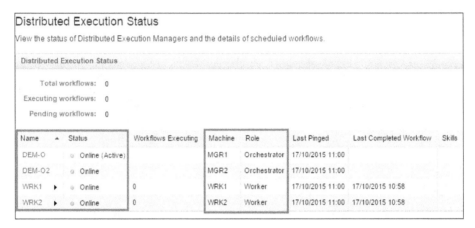

Failover of DEM Worker and proxy agent

Both DEM Worker and the proxy agents follow the active-active HA configuration and failover process is automatic.

DEM Worker

If the worker service stops or loses its connection to the repository (Model Manager Web), the DEM Orchestrator clears all the associated workflow instances to the nonfunctional DEM Worker, thus allowing the other DEM Workers to pick up the workflow. This explains why the failover process is seamless and fluid without the requirement of any extra steps for it to function during and after the failover.

Proxy agents

If you have more than one vCenter endpoints, then you have to install an additional vSphere Agent. It's a 1:1 mapping between the vCenter endpoint and vSphere Agent. You can have multiple agents talking to the same vCenter endpoint in case of high availability but each agent should be on a different server, and they all should have the same name; otherwise, you will run into many issues. For example, if you have three agents pointing to a single vCenter Server, then all the three agents pointing to this vCenter Server should be named as *Agent*.

Please refer to *kb.vmware.com/kb/2052062* for additional details. There are no extra steps required for the failover process.

Summary

Since the HA design holds a significant purpose in the vRealize automation distributed architecture, concluding that the failover test has been a success is an absolute step before endorsing it as a production-ready setup.

Testing the failover for every component is mandatory and the recipe for a successful failover is to follow the steps in a logical sequence for CAFÉ and Manager Service as described in this chapter. The failovers of other components are straightforward and does not require special instructions during and after the failover.

If you want to track the failure component, I would recommend the following approach:

- Check in the load balancer pool setting if the required nodes are in the **UP** state
- Corroborate whether the expected health monitor string is received by surfing the health monitor URL for every component behind the load balancer
- Exercise the health monitor URL against the nodes directly bypassing the load balancer, especially for the component that has the active-passive HA design

Overall, the preceding approach should help you to narrow down the failure service, and further troubleshooting will be additionally required to accurately pinpoint the failure component.

Recognize that the failover of every component should be tested with a successful outcome before endorsing the operation as a grand accomplishment.

In the next chapter, we will look at how to configure an Orchestrator appliance in the HA failover mode behind the NSX load balancer. While there are many documents that talk about Orchestrator, our focus will be a step-by-step guide on configuration.

7
vRealize Orchestrator in High Availability via the NSX Load Balancer

While there are countless public documents that talk about the goodness of vRealize Orchestrator, we wanted to pivot our discussion on high availability configuration via the NSX load balancer for vRealize Orchestrator in this chapter. VMware vRealize Orchestrator (formerly known as VMware vCenter Orchestrator) can be configured to work in two server modes: standalone and cluster. To increase the availability of the VMware vRealize Orchestrator services both in standalone and cluster mode, you can put the Orchestrator behind a load balancer.

Starting with vRO 5.5, clustering has been included as an out-of-box option that enables greater availability for the Orchestrator engine. If an active Orchestrator server becomes unavailable midway through a workflow run, another active or the standby Orchestrator node will take over and complete the workflow without any service interruptions. However, we have two known limitations while configuring the Orchestrator cluster mode:

- Cannot be configured with an embedded database
- Cannot use the embedded directory service

In this chapter, we will talk about the following:

- Types of Orchestrator configuration
- Certificate creation process

- Orchestrator cluster configuration
  - ◦ Preparing the database
  - ◦ Configuring the first Orchestrator server
  - ◦ Configuring the second and third Orchestrator server nodes
  - ◦ Configuring the NSX load balancer

Types of Orchestrator configuration

Clustered Orchestrator servers guarantee high availability and load balancing to protect production installations, such as vRealize Automation.

The Orchestrator can be configured in two modes:

- Active-Active
- Active-Standby

Active-Active

Active nodes are the Orchestrator server instances that run workflows and respond to client requests. If an active Orchestrator node stops responding, it is replaced by one of the inactive Orchestrator server instances:

- All nodes in the cluster are active and provide concurrent connections to the sessions
- There is no service interruption because if one node fails, then the other active nodes keep the client session active
- Workflows should be first created in standalone mode and then imported after configuring the Orchestrator in active–active cluster mode
- The maximum number of nodes in active state is five

Active-Standby

In active-standby configuration, at least one node will be in standby state:

- If the standby node does not receive the heartbeat from the active node for the configured timeout, then it becomes active
- If the Orchestrator client logs into the standby node, then it will throw an error and you have to log in to the active node and the workflow will run through that node

- The maximum number of nodes in active state is five
- The maximum number of nodes in standby state is three

Planning and preparing

Here are some of the key tasks before we start the actual implementation:

- **Software**: Download VMware vRealize Orchestrator OVA to a file share within the target datacenter.

- **Hostnames and IP address planning**: Based on your enterprise naming convention, list the hostname and IP address for vRO nodes including the virtual IP in the load balancer.

- **SSL certificate generation**: Signed or self-signed certificates should be created to contain the Orchestrator virtual IP and the Orchestrator node's hostnames in the **SubjectAltNames** section. This allows traffic to be served by the load balancer without throwing SSL errors. We will leverage a certification generation tool for this task; refer to— kb.vmware.com/kb/2107816.

- **Create DNS entries**: FQDNs will be used throughout our installation. Manually create a record (*forward lookup*) and a *PTR* record (*reverse lookup*) for Linux-based VMware virtual appliances and load balancer virtual addresses.

- **Load balancer configuration**: Commonly used *one-armed* load balancer topology will be configured. Create node entries, virtual addresses (VIPs).

- **Microsoft SQL Server**: We will be leveraging the MSSQL database node to create the Orchestrator database. Windows Clustering is desirable in order to meet availability objectives at the database level and is not covered here as it's beyond the scope of this book.

Infrastructure details

In our setup, we will be configuring three vRealize Orchestrator nodes—two active nodes and one standby node:

Hostname	IP address	Service
vRO.PKCT.LOCAL	10.112.103.127	The virtual IP for the Orchestrator in load balancer
vRO1.PKCT.LOCAL	10.112.103.128	The first vRO node
vRO2.PKCT.LOCAL	10.112.103.129	The second vRO node

Bill of materials

Here is the summary of the Orchestrator versions and build numbers used in this chapter:

- vRealize Orchestrator 6.0.3 build 3000579
- Existing vRealize Automation infrastructure including the NSX load balancer service

Generating Orchestrator certificates

Please refer to the *Creating certificates* section in *Chapter 2, Distributed Installation Using Custom Certificates* to generate the certificates using Certgen tools (`http://kb.vmware.com/kb/2107816` for vRealize Orchestrator).

1. Create a file, `servers.txt`, and add the list of servers for which certificates need to be created:

2. Follow the instructions in step 2 and 3 as mentioned in *Chapter 2, Distributed Installation Using Custom Certificates* under the *Creating certificates* section.

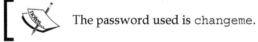 The password used is changeme.

Once the script finishes successfully, it will load the screen with the instructions on how to upload the certificates for all the components. However, at this time, we are interested only in vRO – the following screenshot is pertinent to the Orchestrator:

```
JKS for vRealize Orchestrator (vCO)
-----------------------------------
File: /root/Certificates/vRO_Certificate/jssecacerts
Installation Method:
Copy jssecacerts to /etc/vco/app-server/security/ on each vCO appliance and run the following commands:
chmod 600 /etc/vco/app-server/security/jssecacerts
chown vco:vco /etc/vco/app-server/security/jssecacerts
vcac-config vco-configure (embedded vCAC version only)
service vco-configurator restart
service vco-server restart
```

Copy the `jssecacerts` file to the `/tmp` directory of all the Orchestrator appliances.

This concludes the steps involved in generating the certificate for the Orchestrator. Let's move forward to install and configure the vRO appliance.

Configuring the vRealize Orchestrator cluster

The Orchestrator cluster provides not only high availability, but also load balancing when configured with NSX or another third-party load balancer. Orchestrator clustering is a zero-touch configuration, which means that the Orchestrator cluster is managing itself. The maximum number of active nodes that you define in the configuration dictates how many nodes are switched from standby to running. For example:

- You define the number of active nodes as two; however, you configure three Orchestrator installations in this cluster and power them all on. This would result in two nodes being active and one being in standby mode.

- If you now proceed to power off one of the active nodes, the standby node will become active. You could test this by setting the number of active nodes to 1 in the setup we are about to build.

There are certain drawbacks you should be aware of. It is not recommended to use the Orchestrator client to connect to the nodes running in a cluster. This is done on purpose to make sure that changes to workflows don't occur.

Configuring the setup

We will be configuring two vRealize Orchestrator appliances with both the nodes in active configuration. Since the configuration includes cluster mode, using an external database and authentication (SSO) server is mandatory. The VMware Identity Manager appliance will be used as our SSO server and MSSQL server will be used for the database.

Configuring the Orchestrator to work with an external authentication enables AD users to log in to the Orchestrator client. As SSO is now a highly integrated part of vSphere, using the Orchestrator with AD (or LDAP) isn't really a good solution any longer. SSO can proxy multiple AD and/or LDAP domains and lets you integrate the Orchestrator directly into vCenter as well as other corner pieces of VMware software offerings, making SSO integration a better choice for the future.

Before we explore further, let's add our PKCT.LOCAL domain with the default vRA Tenant (vsphere.local):

1. Log in as administrator@vsphere.local to the vRA default tenant page — https://CAFE.PKCT.LOCAL/vcac and click on the **vsphere.local** tenant:

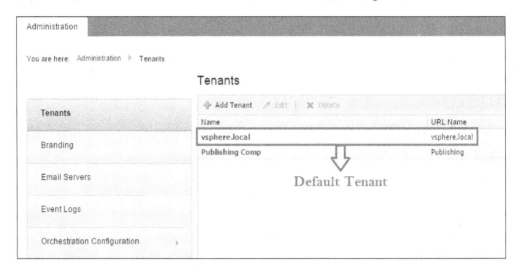

2. Navigate to the **Identity Stores** tab, click **Add Identity Stores**, and fill the field as applicable to your setup; click **Test Connection**, click **Add**, and click **Update**. Please use this screenshot as reference:

This concludes the step of adding an AD domain (PKCT.LOCAL) to the default tenant.

Prerequisites

Before we set out to begin our implementation, gathering and completing the prerequisites are an important task. Let's review each item:

- Allocate the hostname, IP address, and create DNS records (A and PTR) for the vRO virtual IP in the load balancer and two vRO nodes (vRO1, vRO2)

Creating NSX load balancer configurations for CAFÉ

1. Freshly deploy three VMware vRealize Orchestrator appliances without any configurations. (*I'm not going to walk through the OVA deployment in this book.*)
2. Power on and perform the following checks in every Orchestrator appliance.
3. Connect to the VAMI page of the virtual appliance — `https://<IP_address-or_FQDN-of-vRO(1,2)-appliance>:5480`.
4. Navigate to **Network | Address**:
    - Check whether the hostname and DNS entries are accurate.
    - IP settings should be set to static.
5. Navigate to **Admin | Admin** and check whether the SSH is enabled and **Status** shows **Running**.
6. Navigate to **Admin | Time Settings** and ensure that the NTP settings are pointing to your infrastructure NTP server.
7. SSH into the virtual appliance as root user and check whether you are able to ping the virtual IP of vRO in the load balancer and the infrastructure management virtual machines (AD, DNS) using FQDN.
8. If all the preceding steps are true for both the vRO appliances, move on to the next step.

How to do it

While we have multiple sections, here is the flow of steps:

1. Preparing the database
2. Configuring the first Orchestrator server
3. Configuring the second and third Orchestrator server nodes
4. Configuring the NSX load balancer

Preparing the database

Create a database, vCOdb, in the SQL Server and execute the following SQL query to set the following two settings on the Orchestrator database:

In this example, the Orchestrator database is called vCOdb:

```
ALTER DATABASE vCOdb SET READ_COMMITTED_SNAPSHOT ON
ALTER DATABASE vCOdb SET ALLOW_SNAPSHOT_ISOLATION ON
```

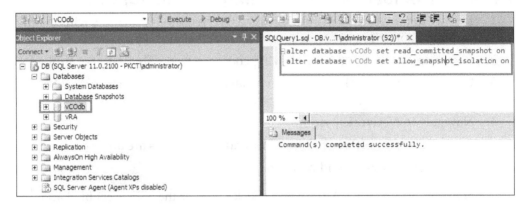

Configuring the first Orchestrator server

In this section, we will configure the first Orchestrator appliance and prepare it for cluster configuration.

The Orchestrator configuration page

Log in to the Orchestrator configuration page (https://vRO1.PKCT.LOCAL:8283) as the vmware user:

1. Key in the password that was provided while deploying the Orchestrator appliance.

2. Locate **Network**, set **IP address** from the drop-down menu, and click **Apply changes**.

Configuring the database

In this section, we will be configuring the Orchestrator appliance with an external database:

1. Navigate to **Database** and fill in the details as applicable to your setup (the following screenshot can be used as reference) and click **Apply changes**.

2. Once you get the message, **Database configuration saved successfully. Create the database tables by clicking the following link**, click the **Create the database tables** link:

Configuring certificates

The certificates that were created via the Certgen tool in the beginning of this chapter will be used in this section. This is an important step, and I would recommend that you read the steps carefully before you start the process. As a disclaimer, I want to highlight that a simple mistake can push your appliance to a flawed state:

1. Using PuTTY, make an SSH connection to the Orchestrator appliance and authenticate using the root credentials.

2. Back up the exiting Java key store file using the following command:

   mv /etc/vco/app-server/security/jssecacerts /etc/vco/app-server/ security/jssecacerts-old

3. Move the `jssecacerts` file from the `/tmp` directory into the `/etc/vco/app-server/security` location using the following command:

```
mv /tmp/jssecacerts /etc/vco/app-server/security
```

4. Execute the following commands to ensure the permission on this file is appropriate; otherwise, the appliance might not be able to start correctly:

```
chmod 600 /etc/vco/app-server/security/jssecacerts

chown vco:vco /etc/vco/app-server/security/jssecacerts
```

5. Reboot the vRealize Orchestrator appliance by running the following command:

```
reboot
```

```
login as: root
VMware vRealize Orchestrator Appliance
root@vRO1.PKCT.LOCAL's password:
Last login: Thu Dec 10 20:20:46 IST 2015 from vidm.pkct.local on ssh
Last login: Thu Dec 10 20:21:22 2015 from ad-pkct.pkct.local
vRO1:~ # mv /etc/vco/app-server/security/jssecacerts /etc/vco/app-server/security/jssecacerts-old
vRO1:~ # mv /tmp/jssecacerts /etc/vco/app-server/security/
vRO1:~ # chmod 600 /etc/vco/app-server/security/jssecacerts
vRO1:~ # chown vco:vco /etc/vco/app-server/security/jssecacerts
vRO1:~ # cd /etc/vco/app-server/security
vRO1:/etc/vco/app-server/security # ls -lhtr
total 24K
-rw-------  1 vco vco   32 Aug 20 14:46 clientcerts
-rw-------  1 vco vco 2.2K Dec 10 19:12 jssecacerts-old
-rw-------  1 vco vco 4.2K Dec 10 19:13 sso.keystore
-rw-------  1 vco vco   48 Dec 10 19:14 passwordencryptor.key
-rw-------  1 vco vco 3.9K Dec 10 20:20 jssecacerts
vRO1:/etc/vco/app-server/security # reboot

Broadcast message from root (pts/0) (Thu Dec 10 20:25:21 2015):

The system is going down for reboot NOW!
vRO1:/etc/vco/app-server/security #
```

6. Once the Orchestrator appliance has restarted, confirm that the newly signed certificates are correctly installed. Go to the vRealize Orchestrator configuration page using its FQDN: `https://vRO1.PKCT.LOCAL:8283`.

7. Right-click the padlock on the top-left corner of the URL and click **More Information**:

   ○ Review the certificate and verify that it is signed by the CA authority used by your organization:

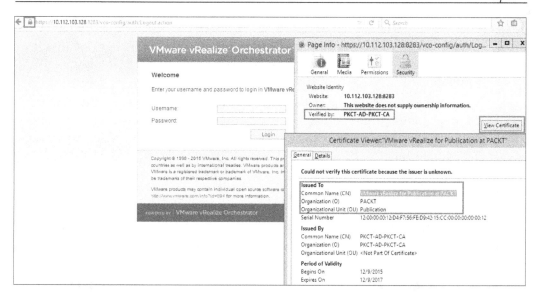

8. If you want to confirm the same from the Java keystore update in the appliance, execute the following command:

```
keytool -list -keystore   /etc/vco/app-server/security/jssecacerts
-v
```

```
login as: root
VMware vRealize Orchestrator Appliance
root@vRO1.PKCT.LOCAL's password:
Last login: Thu Dec 10 20:21:22 IST 2015 from ad-pkct.pkct.local on pts/0
Last login: Thu Dec 10 20:28:42 2015 from ad-pkct.pkct.local
vRO1:~ #
vRO1:~ # keytool -list -keystore /etc/vco/app-server/security/jssecacerts -v
Enter keystore password:

Keystore type: JKS
Keystore provider: SUN

Your keystore contains 1 entry

Alias name: dunes
Creation date: Dec 9, 2015
Entry type: PrivateKeyEntry
Certificate chain length: 2
Certificate[1]:
Owner: CN=VMware vRealize for Publication at PACKT, OU=Publication, O=PACKT, L=BNG, ST=KA, C=IN
Issuer: CN=PKCT-AD-PKCT-CA, DC=PKCT, DC=LOCAL
Serial number: 1200000012d4f756fed94215cc000000000012
Valid from: Wed Dec 09 21:01:06 IST 2015 until: Sat Dec 09 21:11:06 IST 2017
Certificate fingerprints:
        MD5:  0A:5C:2B:05:C8:3D:09:E7:FC:25:D1:47:1D:CA:C9:BD
        SHA1: 40:E1:5A:DC:06:FA:27:E7:96:FE:94:2F:02:23:C6:34:AD:25:0A:2E
        SHA256: C4:9A:3F:91:2A:87:A7:58:B6:88:DE:13:9C:F9:92:49:89:07:4F:EA:1A:BF:80:90:5C:B2:CC:CA:ED:83:EB:29
        Signature algorithm name: SHA256withRSA
        Version: 3
```

 If all goes well, the details in the last two screenshots should match.

Orchestrator server configuration continues

1. On the VMware vRealize Orchestrator configuration login page, log in with the `vmware` username and the password you specified when deploying the appliance.

2. Click the **Network** menu on the left-hand side and navigate to **SSL Trust Manager**, and import and accept the certificate of the SSO server before connecting to an external directory service (URL — `https://vIDM.PKCT.LOCAL:7444`; if you are using PSC, then append the `443` port instead of `7444`).

> For each system you want the vRealize Orchestrator appliance to interact with, enter the target system and click **Import** in the URL section to import the certificate. Ensure to configure a vCenter Server if you want to export the license into Orchestrator.

3. Click the **Authentication** menu on the left-hand side and select **SSO Authentication** as **Authentication mode**. Type the SSO server host without the port number followed by its credentials and click **Register Orchestrator**.

4. Under **SSO Configuration**, set **SSO domain** and **vRO Admin** as applicable to your setup (the following screenshot can be used as reference) and click **Accept Orchestrator Configuration**.

> We were able to list the `pkct.local` domain in the **SSO domain** field since we added the domain to the default tenant in the earlier step.

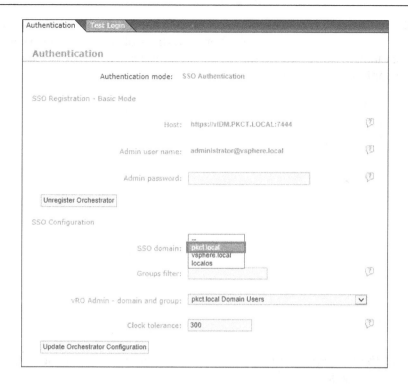

 It is recommended to create a user for vRO purposes in the PKCT.LOCAL directory services. I have created a user, vroadmin, in the PKCT.LOCAL directory services.

5. Navigate to the **Test Login** tab to validate the login. If for some reason you receive the error **The User is not allowed to log in**, and if you have validated all the steps, reboot the Orchestrator appliance and perform the same test—this happened in my setup and the reboot resolved it:

6. Navigate to the **Licenses** menu on the left-hand side and select **Use vCenter Server license**. Fill in the FQDN or IP address of the vCenter server in the **Host** textbox followed by the server credentials. Click **Apply Changes** for the configuration to take effect:

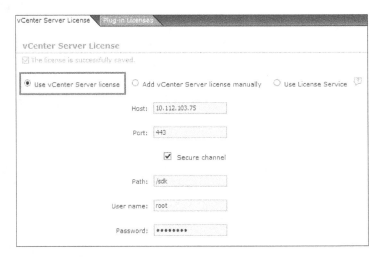

7. Click the **Startup Options** menu on the left-hand side and click **Start service** to restart the service:

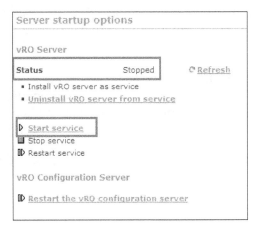

Installing the Orchestrator client

The Orchestrator client interface is designed for the developers who have administrative rights and want to develop workflows, actions, and other custom elements. If you want to use the Orchestrator client to connect to the Orchestrator server not through the Java Web Start but to have the client installed on your local machine, you must download and install the Orchestrator client. In this section, we will take a look at how to install the Orchestrator client:

1. Go to the vRealize Orchestrator management console using its FQDN: `https://vRO.PKCT.LOCAL:8281/vco`.

2. Either click **Start Orchestrator Client** (this requires Java to work) or **Download Orchestrator Client Installable** (full installer depending on the client OS version):

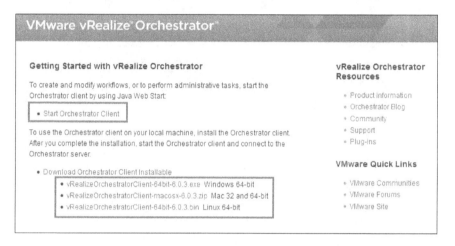

3. Once the Orchestrator client is installed, launch the client and use the `vroadmin@pkct.local` user to log in. Since you are logging in for the first time using the client, you should be presented with the **Certificate Warnings** screen. View, verify, and install any certificates that are shown to continue further:

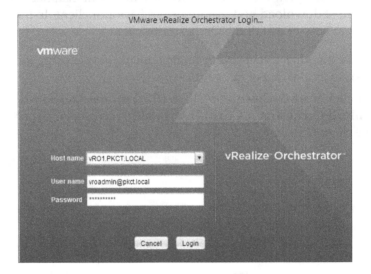

4. Once you are able to successfully log in to the Orchestrator server using the client, go back to the Orchestrator configuration page. (`https://vRO1.PKCT.LOCAL:8283`).

Installing plugins

Since vRealize Automation (vRA) is deemed to become the central cornerstone in the VMware automation effort, vRealize Orchestrator (vRO) is used by vRA to interact with and automate VMware and non VMware products and infrastructure elements. This requires us to install the vRA plugin (`o11nplugin-vcac-6.2.0-2287231.vmoapp`):

1. Click the **Plug-ins** menu and scroll to the bottom of the list.
2. Click the magnifying glass icon to browse to the vRA plugin file and click **Upload and install**:
    ◦   Click **I accept the terms and of the license agreement**
    ◦   Click **Apply changes**

3. Reboot the vRealize Orchestrator appliance and confirm that the installation is **OK** for the new plugins.

Configuring the cluster

To increase the availability of the Orchestrator services, you can configure a cluster of Orchestrator server instances. An Orchestrator cluster consists of at least two Orchestrator server instances that share one database.

To work properly in the cluster, all the Orchestrator server instances must be configured identically with each other and must have the same plugins installed. After you set up the Orchestrator cluster, do not change the configurations of its nodes:

1. Click the **Server availability** menu and click **Cluster mode**. Set **Number of active nodes** to 2 (as per your design) and click **Apply change**.

2. Click the **Startup options** menu on the left-hand side and click **Restart service** (under vRO Server) to restart the service.

3. Click the **Server Availability** menu. After a few minutes (this can range from 1 to 5 min), you should see the first node appear under **Started cluster nodes** in the **RUNNING** status:

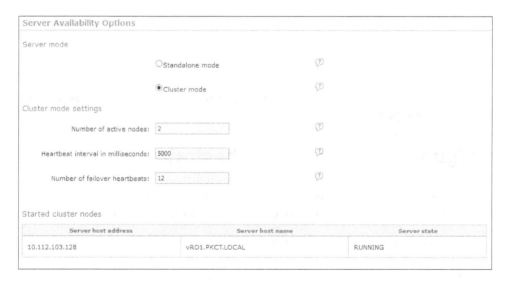

Export configuration

The Orchestrator configuration interface provides a mechanism to export the Orchestrator configuration settings to a local file. This mechanism allows you to take a snapshot of your system configuration at any moment and import this configuration into a new Orchestrator instance:

1. Click the **General** menu and click the **Export Configuration** tab and click **Export**.

2. A configuration file will be exported to the following folder: /var/lib/vco/, in the Orchestrator appliance with the file name, vmo_config_xxxxxxxxxxx. vmconfig:

3. Copy (using the WinSCP tool) the exported file from this Orchestrator node to a Windows machine where the Orchestrator client is installed.

This successfully concludes cluster node configuration in the first Orchestrator node. Proceed and configure the second node of the cluster.

Configuring the second Orchestrator server

Things are going to be easy from now on since you already have hands-on experience of configuring the first Orchestrator server. The following steps help you to configure the second node of the vRealize Orchestrator cluster:

1. Perform the steps detailed in the *Configuring certificates* section.

 Do not perform the steps detailed in the section, *Preparing the database.*

2. On the **VMware vRealize Orchestrator Configuration** login page, log in with the vmware username and the password that you specified when you deployed the appliance.

3. Click the **General** menu and then click the **Import Configuration** tab.

4. Click the magnifying glass icon, browse to the local file system location where the exported file was saved, and click **Import**.

5. Click the **Network** menu on the left-hand side and click the **Network** tab:

   ° From the **IP address** drop-down menu, select the IP address of the second appliance since the DNS name will be set to the FQDN of the first node and click **Apply changes**.

6. Continue to follow the steps detailed in the *Installing the plugins* section:

   ° It is important to ensure that the same version and plugins are installed on both nodes.

7. Click the **Server Availability** menu. After a few minutes, you should see the second node appear under the **Started cluster nodes RUNNING** status:

Configuring the NSX load balancer

This section only describes the load balancing aspect of the NSX product configuration, assuming that NSX has already been configured and validated to work properly on the target environment or networks:

1. Log in to vCenter Server where NSX has been configured.

2. Navigate to **Home | Networking & Security | NSX Edges** and select the **Edge appliance** deployed for the use of a distributed vRealize Automation installation.

3. Navigate to **Manage** | **Settings** and select the **Interfaces** menu on the left-hand side.

4. Select the first vNIC and click the **Edit** button. This will be your load balancer virtual appliance.

5. Click the **Add** button to assign a static IP address (virtual IP for Orchestrator) to the virtual interface.

Orchestrator NSX load balancer configurations

In this section, we will be configuring an application profile, service monitoring, pool and virtual server settings in the NSX load balancer server for the Orchestrator cluster to work behind a load balancer.

Configuring an application profile

1. Log in to vCenter Server where NSX has been set up.

2. Navigate to **Home** | **Networking & Security** | **NSX Edges** and select your previously created NSX edge.

3. On the **Load Balancer** tab select the **Application Profiles** menu.

4. Click the **Add** button to create a new profile and complete the form according to the following table:

Name	Type	Enable SSL passthrough	Persistence
vRO	HTTPS	Checked	None

Configuring service monitors

1. Log in to vCenter Server where NSX has been set up.

2. Navigate to **Home** | **Networking & Security** | **NSX Edges** and select your previously created NSX edge.

3. In the **Load Balancer** tab, select the **Service Monitoring** menu on the left-hand side.

4. Click the **Add** button to create a new monitor and complete the form according to the following table:

Name	Interval	Timeout	Retries	Type	Method	URL	Receive
vRO_SM_8281	3	15	3	HTTPS	GET	/vco/api/docs/index.html	200

Configuring pools

1. Log in to vCenter Server where NSX has been set up.

2. Navigate to **Home | Networking & Security | NSX Edges** and select your previously created NSX edge.

3. In the **Load Balancer** tab, select **Pools**.

4. Click on the **Add** button to create a new pool and complete the form according to the following table:

Pool name	Algorithm	Monitors	Member name	Example IP address	Port	Monitor port
vRO_POOL	Round Robin	vRO_SM_8281	vRO1	10.112.103.128	8281	8281
N/A	N/A	N/A	vRO2	10.112.103.129	8281	8281

 Before configuring the **Virtual Servers**, ensure both the members are enabled and are in the **UP** status under **Show Pool Statistics**.

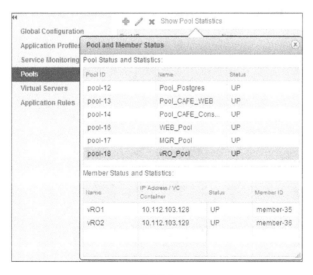

Configuring virtual servers

1. Log in to vCenter Server where NSX has been set up.

2. Navigate to **Home | Networking & Security | NSX Edges** and select your previously created NSX edge.

3. In the **Load Balancer** tab, select **Virtual Servers**.

4. Click on the **Add** button to create a new virtual server and complete the form according to the following table:

Application profile	Name	IP address	Protocol	Port	Default pool
vRO	vRO_LB_8281	10.112.103.126	HTTPS	8281	vRO_POOL

We need to perform one last step before we conclude that the vRO load balancer configuration is complete. Open IE browser and connect to the vRO service monitoring URL – `https://vRO.PKCT.LOCAL:8281/vco/api/docs/index.html` and check whether you see the Orchestrator API page.

 The FQDN, `vRO.PKCT.LOCAL`, is the Orchestrator virtual IP in the load balancer.

VREALIZE ORCHESTRATOR API

REST   Data Model   Files and Libraries

⌂ Home

REST Resources

This API supports a Representational State Transfer (REST) model for accessing a set of resources through a fixed set of operations. The following resources are accessible through the RESTful model:

*   Actions Service
*   Catalog Service
*   Category Service
*   Configuration Service
*   Content Service
*   Inventory Service
*   Packages Service
*   Plugin Service
*   Resource Service
*   Server Configuration Service
*   Service Descriptor Service
*   Tagging Service
*   Task Service
*   User Interaction Service

This concludes the NSX load balancer configuration.

At this stage, connect to Orchestrator using the Orchestrator client with the load balancer virtual IP:

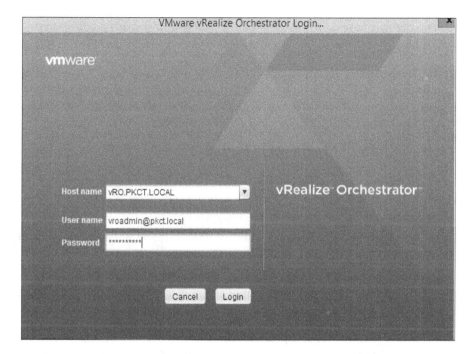

 In case you don't see all the folders under Library once you log in, log out and browse to the first Orchestrator node—https://vRO1.PKCT.LOCAL:8283.

1. Navigate to **Startup Options** and click the **Stop** service.
2. Navigate to **Troubleshooting** and click the **Reset current version** link.
3. Once the preceding step is successful, navigate to **Startup Options** and click **Start service**.

Repeat the preceding three steps in the second Orchestrator node. This should help solve the issue.

vRealize Orchestrator high availability mechanism

VMware vRealize Orchestrator nodes update their heartbeat in the database every 5 seconds. The default number of missed heartbeats that indicates a problem on a node is 3 heartbeats.

If a vRealize Orchestrator node has a problem and stops the heartbeat, vRealize Orchestrator is aware that its heartbeat has stopped. When the heartbeat entry in the database is not updated, other vRealize Orchestrator nodes in the cluster will know that the heartbeat of the node with a problem has stopped.

When the timeout is reached, the following happens:

- The vRealize Orchestrator node with the problem disappears from the **Started Cluster Nodes** section under the **Server Availability** option in the Orchestrator configuration page
- The other vRealize Orchestrator nodes in the cluster determine that it is nonresponsive and take over the workflows
- Once the server is ready to be brought online after fixing the issue, it's recommended to restart the impacted Orchestrator appliance or at least, restart the `vco-server` and `vco-configurator` services

Workflow continues from the last point of execution when the vRealize Orchestrator node is started. This mechanism provides the vRealize Orchestrator workflow HA.

If the default heartbeat timeout is considered too sensitive, you can increase the heartbeat timeout:

1. Stop all the vRealize Orchestrator server nodes.

2. In the cluster configuration tab of the Orchestrator configuration interface, change the value of the number of failover heartbeats from 3 to a higher number for every vRealize Orchestrator server node. The values should be the same for all the nodes in the cluster.

3. Start all the vRealize Orchestrator server nodes one by one.

While writing the workflows, ensure that in the event of a failover, the building block of that workflow (for example, scriptable) task should rerun when the workflow resumes on the failover vRealize Orchestrator node.

Configuring vRO at CAFÉ or IaaS makes a difference!

Before we conclude this chapter, I want to talk about how vRO can be leveraged depending on the use case:

- **Use case 1**: For instance, if you want to automate any post provisioning operations, then you may want to add vRO at the CAFÉ layer. This enables to create Anything as a Service (XaaS) by exposing the service blueprint to the customers utilizing the power of vRealize Orchestrator (vRO) called Advanced Service Designer. You will see more about ASD in the next chapter.

- **Use case 2**: The Orchestrator can be configured as an endpoint at the IaaS level if you would like to provision or decommission a machine, especially for mission-critical systems that typically require interactions with a number of different management systems including DNS servers, load balancers, CMDBs, IP address management, and other systems.

 For additional details, I would encourage you to read – `http://pubs.vmware.com/vra-62/topic/com.vmware.vra.extensibility.doc/GUID-F47DD779-F96F-4DA8-9697-D9A88B115866.html`.

Summary

The primary purpose of this chapter was to explain the detailed steps involved in creating a vRealize Orchestrator cluster behind an NSX load balancer. Infrastructure as a Service (IaaS) represents the deployment and life cycle management of server workloads – whether they are a traditional vSphere virtual machine in an organization's internal private cloud, a cloud workload in VMware vCloud Air, Microsoft Azure, Amazon Workspace Services, or another provider, or even physical servers. Anything as a Service (XaaS) represents virtually anything else that isn't IaaS. vRO enables XaaS inside vRA. The relationship between the two works like this – vRA is the request and approval portal, vRO is the orchestration engine.

In the next chapter, you will read about the power of Advanced Service Designer and how it can be leveraged to create XaaS.

8
The Power of Advanced Service Designer (ASD)

So far, we have dealt with Infrastructure as a Service (a.k.a. IaaS) where we utilized the capability of vRealize Automation to provision a machine, perform day-to-day operations, and so on. If you would like to create a customized service along with the IaaS service that is available in vRA, a new powerful feature called **Advanced Service Designer (ASD)** is your answer. It also provides the ability to create **Anything as a Service (XaaS)** by exposing the service blueprint to customers utilizing the power of **vRealize Orchestrator (vRO)**.

ASD is a part of vRA that allows you to extend IaaS operations, as well as provide service offerings to users. It works with vRO and basically anything that vRO can do, can be made available to the user through their catalog.

You can consider vRA as a waiter taking orders from the user, and the catalog is the menu. Once the user has made their selection, it is sent to the cook (vRO) to perform the work and return the finished product, in some cases the item.

In this chapter, we will focus our discussion on the following topics:

- An ASD overview
- Enabling and configuring ASD
- What is a service blueprint
- Creating custom resources
- Creating resource action

Advanced Service Designer overview

Advanced Service Designer is made up of the ASD provider, which does the work, and the ASD UI, which provides an interface for the administration and creation of the custom resources/blueprints and day 2 actions.

There are three main roles involved with Advanced Service Designer:

- **Tenant administrator**: Responsible for adding the vRO endpoint so that it can be used by ASD
- **Service architect**: Creates all the ASD Custom Resources/Blueprints and Day 2 Actions
- **Consumer/user**: Consumes the ASD blueprints that have been published to the Catalog

The ASD provider mainly talks to the:

- **Catalog**, either to initiate a request or provide information
- **vRO** to invoke a workflow, which supports the service blueprint:

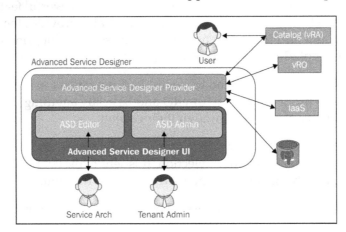

Advanced Service Designer provides a way for the service architects to create advanced custom services and publish them as catalog items. They can provide custom resource-types mapped to vRealize Orchestrator object-types and define them as items to be provisioned by creating blueprints. These are termed as **service blueprints**, and these can be published as catalogs by mapping them to specific services and can be entitled to specific business groups. For example, you can provide a service such as provisioning a VLAN as a service for the network operations team, backup as service to back up a database for database administrators, and provide an ability to create/modify an AD account as a service for infrastructure administrator.

Also, ASD provides a way to take actions on the items provisioned by sources other than Advanced Service Designer. These additional actions a.k.a. resource actions are connected with vRO workflows and will execute the actions on the provisioned items. To utilize such capabilities, create a resource mapping that corresponds to resource types in vRealize Orchestrator.

Enabling the ASD tab in vRA

Enabling ASD is an easy task. However, two mandatory prerequisites should be fulfilled for it to work:

- Designated users or a common group should be enabled with the **Service Architect** role
- The vRealize Automation license (CAFÉ appliance) should be licensed with either **Advanced** or **Enterprise**

ADS is not available in the Standard edition.

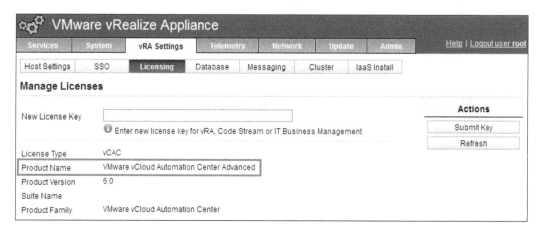

Granting the service architect role

There are two ways you can assign the service architect role:

- Assign to a specific identity store user/group
- Assign to a custom group

Assigning to a specific user

1. Log into the Publishing portal (`https://CAFE.PKCT.LOCAL/vcac/org/Publishing`) as a tenant administrator and navigate to **Administration | Identity Store Users & Groups**; enter the designated user name, select the user, check the **Service Architect** role, and click **Update**:

2. Log out the tenant administrator user and log in as an ASD user. If the preceding step is successful, the **Advanced Services** tab should be visible for this user:

Creating a custom group and assigning the role

1. Log in as a tenant administrator and navigate to **Administration | Custom Groups**.

2. Click **Add**, type a name for **Custom Group**, select the **Service Architect** role, and click **Next**.

3. In the **Members** tab, type the user's name who needs to be a part of the **Service Architect** group and click **Add**.

4. Once the preceding task is complete, log out the tenant administrator and log in as the ASD user.

5. If the preceding step is successful, the **Advanced Services** tab should be visible for this user.

Configuring the advanced service endpoints (vRealize Orchestrator)

It is important to configure the vRO server since ASD actions are performed using the vRO plugins and workflows that are provided and supported by the Orchestrator server. You can either utilize the embedded vRO or configure the external vRO. In this exercise, let's see how to configure an external Orchestrator endpoint.

Who can configure the ASD?

System (administrator@vsphere.local) and tenant administrators can configure vRealize Automation to use an external vRealize Orchestrator server. In addition, system administrators can also determine the workflow folders that are available to each tenant. Tenant administrators can configure the vRealize Orchestrator plugins as endpoints and import workflow packages.

1. Log into the default tenant (https://CAFE.PKCT.LOCAL/vcac) as tenant administrator and navigate to **Administration | Orchestration Configuration | Server Configuration**:

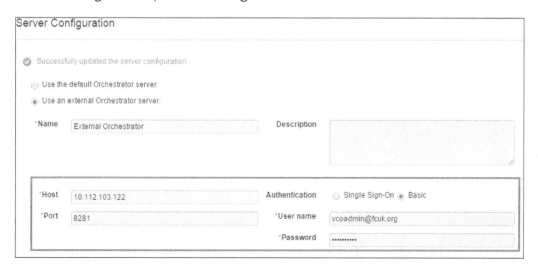

If you select the **Use the default Orchestrator server** option, then the Orchestrator server configured in the default tenant (`https://CAFE.PKCT.LOCAL/vcac`) will be used.

Service blueprint

A catalog in vRealize Automation is referred to as a service blueprint in ASD terminology. While a blueprint is a complete specification of a service, with service blueprints, you can publish predefined and custom vRealize Orchestrator workflows as catalog items to either request or provision. Depending on whether or not you would like to perform any actions after provisioning, the steps involved in creating a service blueprint will vary:

- Perform actions on the service blueprint after it is provisioned:

    Required steps are:

    1. Create a custom resource mapping.
    2. Create a service blueprint.
    3. Create resource actions that define the post provisioning operations.

- No actions are required after provisioning a service blueprint:

    Required step is:

    1. Create a service blueprint.

Prerequisites

Configure the vCenter Server in vRO using the Orchestrator client:

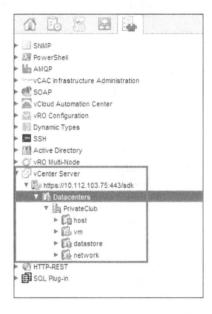

Ensure the Orchestrator server configuration is set up for the tenant (publishing).

Service blueprint provisioning and post-provisioning operation

In this exercise, we will presume that the requirement is to provision a service blueprint and perform actions post provisioning. For demonstration purposes, we will create a service blueprint to create a datacenter in the vCenter endpoint.

As mentioned earlier, it is a three step process:

1. Create a custom resource mapping.
2. Create a service blueprint.
3. Create resource actions that define the post provisioning operations.

Creating a custom resource

To create an advanced service and allow your consumers to provision items, you must first create a custom resource that defines the item to be provisioned:

- You create a custom resource to define a new type of provisioned item and map it to an existing vCenter Orchestrator object type.

- The vCenter Orchestrator object types are the objects exposed through the APIs of the vCenter Orchestrator plugins.

- The custom resource is the output type of a provisioning workflow and can also be the input type for a resource action workflow.

- For example if you have a running vCenter Server instance and you also have the vCenter Server plug-in configured to work with vCenter Orchestrator, all of the object types from the vCenter Server API are exposed in vCenter Orchestrator.

- In addition, the vCenter Server plugin exposes the vSphere inventory objects in the vCenter Orchestrator inventory.

- The vSphere inventory objects include data centers, folders, ESXi hosts, virtual machines and appliances, resource pools, and so on. You can perform various operations on these objects. For example, you can create, clone, or destroy virtual machines.

Let's see how this works:

1. Log in to the vRA self-service portal as the user who has the **Service Architect** role and is added to the **Business Groups**. I have configured the ASD user with the service architect role and added them to the Publishing BG business group:

2. Navigate to **Advanced Services** | **Custom Resources** and click **Add**.

 Since our requirement is to create a **Datacenter** in vCenter Server, configure the vCenter Server in Orchestrator to be able to successfully provision this service blueprint.

3. Populate the **Resource type** screen as per the following screenshot and click **Next**:

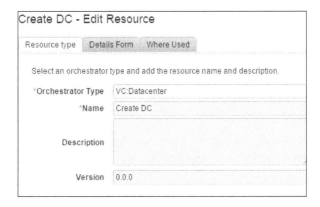

4. Click **Add** in the next screen without making any changes.

Create a service blueprint

1. Navigate to **Service Blueprint**, click **Add**, and select the workflow (**Orchestrator | Library | vCenter | Datacenter**).

2. Select the **Create Datacenter** workflow and click **Next**.

3. Type `Create datacenter` in the **Name** field, add the `1.0.0` version number without quotes and click `Next`.

4. Click **Next** in the **Blueprint Form** page without making any changes.

5. In the **Provisioned Resource** page, select **newDatacenter [Create DC]** from the drop-down menu and click **Add**:

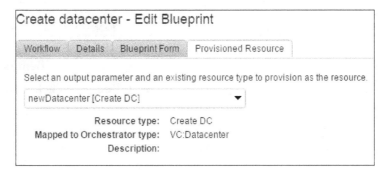

6. Select the service blueprint that we created, **Create datacenter**, and click **Publish**. Now the status should change from **Draft** to **Published**:

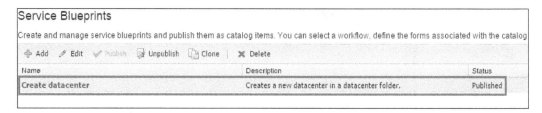

7. Navigate to **Administration | Catalog Management | Services** and create a service with name **DC** and make it **Active**:

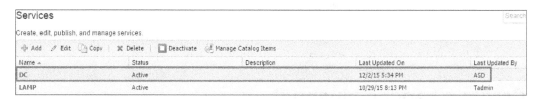

8. Navigate to **Administration | Catalog Management | Catalog Items** and map the DC service to the **Create datacenter** service blueprint (catalog) created in Advanced Service Designer:

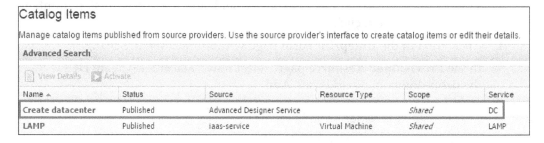

9. Navigate to **Administration | Catalog Management | Entitlements**.

10. Create entitlement by adding **Service, Catalog Item** and click **Add**:

You would not have found any relevant Datacenter action in the Actions section. We will create a custom action using Resource Actions under the Advanced Services tab and map it to Entitled Actions.

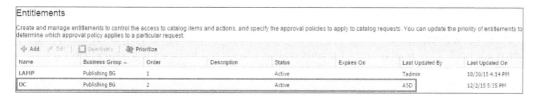

11. Click the **Catalog** tab and you should be able to see the **Create datacenter** service blueprint we just created:

12. Click on **Request** for the **Create datacenter** service blueprint, fill in the required details, and click **Submit**. You should see a datacenter being created in the vCenter endpoint.

13. Navigate to the **Items** tab and you will see the service blueprint provisioned since we chose the **newDatacenter [Create DC]** option in the earlier step. At this stage, we cannot perform any post provisioning actions as we did not find a suitable action for this **Service Catalog** under **Entitled Actions**. Hence, we will create **Resource Action** in the next step and map it:

Creating a resource action

Resource actions are used to create a custom post provisioning action on the items provisioned. This is achieved by publishing vRealize Orchestrator workflows as resource actions:

- To create a resource action for an item provisioned via Advanced Service Designer, configure the custom resource as an input parameter for the workflow

- To create a resource action for an item that is provisioned by a source different from the Advanced Service Designer, configure the resource mapping as an input parameter to the workflow

- When you entitle the **Resource Actions**, they appear in the **Actions** drop-down menu of the provisioned items on the **Items** tab

Let's see how to do this:

1. Navigate to **Advanced Services | Resource Actions** and click **Add**.

2. Select the workflow (**Orchestrator | Library | vCenter | Datacenter**).

3. Select the **Delete datacenter** workflow and click **Next**.

4. Select **Delete DC** for the resource type, set datacenter for **Input** parameter and click **Next**.

5. Fill the **Details** page as shown in the following screenshot and click **Next**:

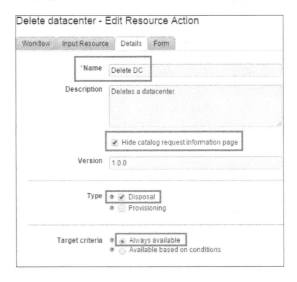

6. Click **Add** in the **Form** page without making any changes.

7. Select **Delete DC** under **Resource Actions** and click **Publish**. Now the status should change from **Draft** to **Published**:

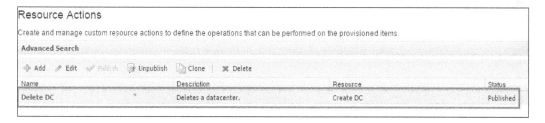

8. Navigate to **Administration | Catalog Management | Entitlements** and click DC to update the **Entitled Actions** for the service blueprint **Create datacenter**:

   1. Click **Next** in the **Details** page without making any changes.

   2. Click the green plus sign next to **Entitled Actions**, select **Delete DC** that was created in **Resource Action**, click **OK** and then click **Update**:

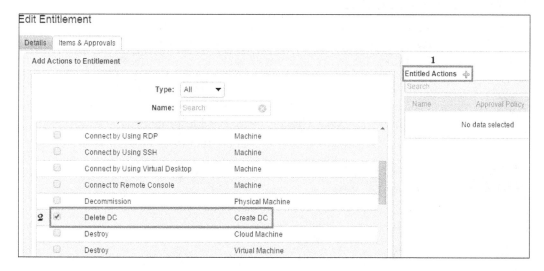

9. Navigate to the **Items** tab, click on the provisioned item (in my setup, it is **First ASD DC**) and you should be able to see the **Delete DC** action for the datacenter that was created earlier:

No actions required after provisioning a service blueprint

In this exercise, we will presume that the requirement is to provision a service blueprint without any actions post provisioning. For demonstration purposes, we will create a service blueprint to provision a virtual machine in the vCenter endpoint:

1. Log in to the vRA self-service portal as the user who has the **Service Architect** role and is added to the **Business Group**. I have configured the ASD user with the service architect role and added them to the **Publishing BG** business group:

2. Navigate to **Advanced Services | Service Blueprints**.

3. Click **Add** and navigate to the workflow (**Orchestrator | Library | vCenter | Virtual Machine Management**):

    1. Select create simple virtual machine workflow and click **Next**.

    2. Type `Create VM` in the **Name** field, add the `1.0.0` version number without quotes and click **Next**.

    3. Click **Next** if you are in the **Blueprint Form** page.

    4. In the **Provisioned Resource** page, click **Add** since the drop-down menu has only one option, **No provisioning**.

4. Select the service blueprint that we created, **Create VM**, and click **Publish**. Now the status should change from **Draft** to **Published**:

5. Navigate to **Administration | Catalog Management | Services** and create the **Create VM** service:

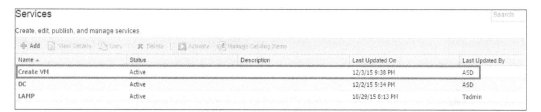

6. Navigate to **Administration | Catalog Management | Catalog Items** and map the **Create VM** service to the **Create VM** service blueprint (catalog) created in Advanced Service Designer:

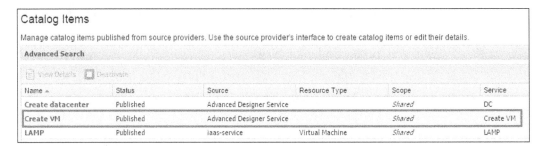

7. Navigate to **Administration | Catalog Management | Entitlements**.
8. Create entitlement by adding **Services** and **Catalog Items** and click **Add**:

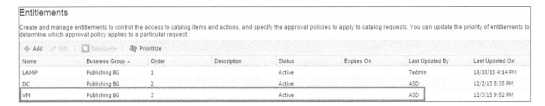

9. Click the **Catalog** tab and you should be able to see the **Create VM** service blueprint we just created:

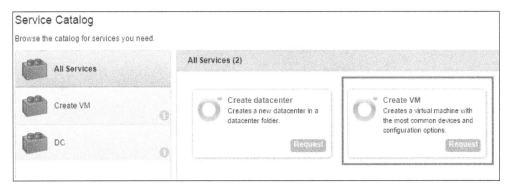

10. Click on **Request** for the **Create VM** service blueprint, fill in the required details, and click **Submit**. You should see the VM created in the vCenter endpoint.

11. Navigate to the **Items** tab and you will not see the service blueprint provisioned since we chose the **no provisioning** option in the earlier step. If you want actions to be performed on the provisioned items, then custom resource mapping should be the first step before configuring the service blueprint.

Summary

This chapter is primarily focused on describing the power of Advanced Service Designer. The combination of ASD and vRealize Orchestrator can create XaaS or Anything as a Service. While we kept our focus on the basics, Advanced Service Design contains instructions on creating the major building blocks of an advanced service, such as resource types, service blueprints, and resource actions. Additionally, information about managing catalog items, organizing them into services, and publishing the services to service catalogs is a huge topic, which is beyond the scope of this book. The examples used in this chapter are quite simple for an effortless understanding. I would encourage you to try more use cases using different workflows once you grab the basics of ASD from this chapter. Happy learning!

Index

D

E

F

G

H

I

N

NSX load balancer configuration
about 40, 173
prerequisite 40
updating, for MGR 82
updating, for vPostgres 49
updating, for WEB 82
NSX load balancer configurations, CAFÉ
about 52
application profile configuration 52
creating 161
pool configuration 53, 58
service monitoring configuration 52, 58
updating 58
virtual servers configuration 53
NSX load balancer configurations, for IaaS MGR
about 74, 94
application profile configuration 74
pool configuration 74, 75, 94
pools statistic, after adding second node 94
service monitoring configuration 74
virtual server configuration 75
NSX load balancer configurations, IaaS WEB
about 64, 65, 89
application profile configuration 65
pool configuration 65, 89
pools statistics, after adding second node 90
service monitoring configuration 65
virtual server configuration 66
virtual server configuration, checkpoint 66
NSX load balancer configurations, vPostgres
about 43-46
application profile configuration 43
pool configuration 43
service monitoring configuration 43
steps 42
virtual server configuration 43
NSX load balancer configuration, vPostgres
pool configuration 49

service monitoring configuration 49
updating 49

O

online DEM Orchestrator
checking 151
Orchestrator
configuring, with external database 162
installing 95-97
Orchestrator client
installing 169, 170
Orchestrator cluster
configuring 171
Orchestrator configuration
about 156
active-active 156
active-standby 156
export configuration settings 172
page 162
planning 157
preparing 157
Orchestrator NSX load balancer configurations
about 174
application profile, configuring 174
pools, configuring 175
service monitors, configuring 174
virtual servers, configuring 176, 177
Orchestrator server
certificates, configuring 163-165
configuring 162-172

P

permissions
providing, in vSphere endpoint 118
PFX certificate
installing, to IIS web server 62, 63
Platform Service Controller (PSC) 6
provision methods
reference link 105
proxy agent
failover 152
installation 78,-82, 98-101
installation, prerequisites 78
setup details 79

R

RabbitMQ 8
RepoUtil commands 11
reservation policies
  configuring 124-128
roles, Advanced Service Designer (ASD)
  consumer/user 182
  service architect 182
  tenant administrator 182
RunOneOnly feature 15

S

second active web node
  installing 89
  installing, prerequisites 89
second DEM Worker
  installing 98, 99
  installing, prerequisites 98
service
  creating 132
service architect role
  assigning, to custom group 184
  assigning, to specific user 184
  granting 183
service blueprints
  about 182, 186
  creating 189-191
  creating, for provisioning virtual
    machine 194-196
  custom resource, creating 188, 189
  post-provisioning operation 187
  prerequisites 187
  provisioning operation 187
  resource action, creating 192-194
service catalog
  creating 118
  requesting 135, 136
shutdown order
  for vRealize Automation components 18
simple deployment architecture 22
Single Sign-On (SSO) 5
Software-Defined Data Center (SDDC) 2
specific user
  service architect role, assigning to 184

SSL certificates 27
standby Manager Service
  installing 93
  installing, prerequisites 93
startup order
  roadmap 16, 17
Subject Alternative Names (SANs) 29
SUSE Linux Enterprise Server 11 (SLES) 7

T

Telemetry 10
template
  VM, converting to 116

U

user
  deployment, monitoring by 136

V

validation test 86-89
vCenter
  VM customization specifications,
    configuring in 128
  VM template specifications,
    configuring in 128
vCloud Automation Center (vCAC) 1
Virtual Machine Observer (VMO) 14
VM
  converting, to template 116
VM customization specifications
  configuring, in vCenter 128
VM template specifications
  configuring, in vCenter 128
vPostgres
  about 7
  contents 7
  failure 141
vRA
  about 2
  ASD tab, enabling in 183
  components 5, 140
  conceptual diagram 5
  key capabilities 3

W

Thank you for buying
Learning VMware vRealize Automation

About Packt Publishing

Packt, pronounced 'packed', published its first book, *Mastering phpMyAdmin for Effective MySQL Management*, in April 2004, and subsequently continued to specialize in publishing highly focused books on specific technologies and solutions.

Our books and publications share the experiences of your fellow IT professionals in adapting and customizing today's systems, applications, and frameworks. Our solution-based books give you the knowledge and power to customize the software and technologies you're using to get the job done. Packt books are more specific and less general than the IT books you have seen in the past. Our unique business model allows us to bring you more focused information, giving you more of what you need to know, and less of what you don't.

Packt is a modern yet unique publishing company that focuses on producing quality, cutting-edge books for communities of developers, administrators, and newbies alike. For more information, please visit our website at www.packtpub.com.

About Packt Enterprise

In 2010, Packt launched two new brands, Packt Enterprise and Packt Open Source, in order to continue its focus on specialization. This book is part of the Packt Enterprise brand, home to books published on enterprise software – software created by major vendors, including (but not limited to) IBM, Microsoft, and Oracle, often for use in other corporations. Its titles will offer information relevant to a range of users of this software, including administrators, developers, architects, and end users.

Writing for Packt

We welcome all inquiries from people who are interested in authoring. Book proposals should be sent to author@packtpub.com. If your book idea is still at an early stage and you would like to discuss it first before writing a formal book proposal, then please contact us; one of our commissioning editors will get in touch with you.

We're not just looking for published authors; if you have strong technical skills but no writing experience, our experienced editors can help you develop a writing career, or simply get some additional reward for your expertise.

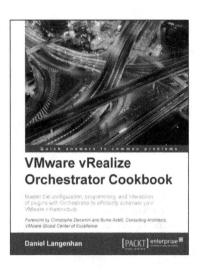

VMware vRealize Orchestrator Cookbook

ISBN: 978-1-78439-224-6   Paperback: 382 pages

Master the configuration, programming, and interaction of plugins with Orchestrator to efficiently automate your VMware infrastructure

1. Program with Orchestrator to automate and synchronize your infrastructure.

2. Integrate the base plug-ins into your workflows.

3. Packed with over 100 example workflows, packaged for download and reuse.

VMware vRealize Operations Performance and Capacity Management

ISBN: 978-1-78355-168-2   Paperback: 276 pages

A hands-on guide to mastering performance and capacity management in a virtual data center

1. Understand the drawbacks of traditional paradigm and management that make performance and capacity management difficult in SDDC.

2. Master the counters in vCenter and vRealize Operations by discovering what they mean and their interdependencies.

3. Build rich dashboards using a practical and easy-to-follow approach supported with real-life examples.

Please check **www.PacktPub.com** for information on our titles

VMware vRealize Orchestrator Essentials

ISBN: 978-1-78588-424-5   Paperback: 184 pages

Get hands-on experience with vRealize Orchestrator and automate your VMware environment

1. Gain an in-depth understanding of vRO in the VMware infrastructure.

2. Create your own advanced vRO scripts using JavaScript.

3. A step-by-step tutorial to manage and create workflows with vRO.

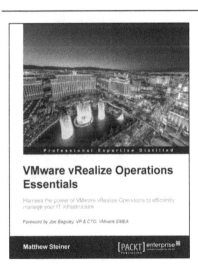

VMware vRealize Operations Essentials

ISBN: 978-1-78528-475-5   Paperback: 302 pages

Harness the power of VMware vRealize Operations to efficiently manage your IT infrastructure

1. Extract the optimum performance, availability, and capacity of your IT infrastructure with the help of vRealise Operations Manager.

2. Leverage the power of strategic reports to drive tactful decision-making within the IT department.

3. A pragmatic guide to proficiently manage your applications and storage.

Please check **www.PacktPub.com** for information on our titles